Austin

a Poem

Austin

a Poem

Dave Oliphant

ALAMO BAY PRESS
SEADRIFT•AUSTIN

Copyright © 2018 by Dave Oliphant

All rights reserved. No part of this book may be reproduced in any form without permission in writing from the publisher, except by a reviewer who may quote brief passages in a review.

Cover illustration: Texas Department of Transportation, 1984; Dolph Briscoe Center for American History, The University of Texas at Austin

Interior illustrations: Sanborn Map Company, 1935; Dolph Briscoe Center for American History, The University of Texas at Austin

Book Design: ABP

For orders and information:
Alamo Bay Press
825 W 11th Ste 114
Austin, Texas 78701
mick@alamobaypress.com
www.alamobaypress.com

Library of Congress Control Number: 2018930413
ISBN: 978-1-943306-10-7

to
Pamela Booton & Lowell Mick White
for encouragement & support
& especially for
this fourth book
from ABP

Contents

xi   Introduction

1   Proem
35   Guadalupe
45   Sabine
69   Red River
85   San Jacinto
99   San Antonio
105   Nueces
123   Rio Grande
137   San Gabriel

189   The Choice

201   About Dave Oliphant

Austin

a Poem

Introduction

Over three decades have now passed since my book-length poem "Austin" first appeared in print, self-published in 1985 under my own imprint, Prickly Pear Press. Fifteen years later, in 2000, Joe Bratcher of Host Publications generously reprinted the Austin poem as part of my *Memories of Texas Towns & Cities*. Prior to the appearance of the *Memories* book, I had revised and corrected "Austin," and over the next fifteen years I continued to correct errors and to change words, lines, and stanzas. Always I have valued the Austin poem more than any single work of mine, even though I also feel a special attachment to *KD: a Jazz Biography*, my other book-length poem, and have held dearest to my heart *María's Book*, my "encyclopedia" of love, as its one reviewer called my collection of 55 poems. Throughout the past thirty-two years, as I kept returning to "Austin," I struggled "to get it right." Paul Válery famously declared that "a poem is never finished, only abandoned," but I found that during all those years I could not leave "Austin" alone. Even after re-reading and tinkering with the poem for such a long period of time, it still may not be "well-made," as one reviewer wrote on its first appearance. Despite its imperfections, "Austin" has remained for me deeply satisfying for some of the reasons that I will here attempt to suggest.

As I have said elsewhere, the Austin poem came about as a natural part of my series of poems on Texas towns and cities. After I had started writing the first of those town and city pieces, beginning in 1974 with "Houston," I knew that I would eventually write on Austin and my many years in the city, from my first remembered visit in 1956, through my wayward years in the 1960s as an undergraduate and graduate student, and following my return in 1976 when I began to teach at the University. Only after I had come back to Austin, with my wife María Isabel and our children Darío and Elisa, did I begin to conceive of a poem on the city and on its namesake, Stephen F. Austin, referred to in "Austin" by his adopted Spanish name, Estevan. My first problem was how to organize what I suspected would be a poem much longer than any of the other pieces in the series, since my plan was to combine the history of the city and the life of Estevan with my own personal life and the lives of fellow students and professors known during my years as a student and later as a teacher and editor. I can no longer recall what led to my decision to divide the poem into eight sections, which, apart from a "Proem," would each be based on one of the river streets that "flows" through the University area. When this framework somehow came to mind, I could see that it would allow me to present something of the history of the capital city and the University, and also of the histories of other places in the State through which the actual rivers course. From early on I had conceived of "Austin" as a type of epic, and thus the river-street structure would serve in fulfilling Pound's definition of the genre as "a poem containing history."

The events and lives evoked in the Austin poem have continued to resonate for me. For this reason I wanted to have a revised, hopefully improved, version of "Austin" available to any reader interested in the subject, now or in the future. In revising "Austin" once again, I was eager to try and make the work the best that I could, especially in light of the fact that the historical figures who appear in its pages contributed so significantly to the city that represents for me and many others an ideal place. The many friends or acquaintances that I made in Austin between 1960 and 1985, and who grace the lines and stanzas of the poem, stand for me in various ways as models of exemplary qualities, which I continue to admire and which influenced my own life and the lives of others. To all those named in "Austin," I owe a truly enduring debt that I have tried to repay, in a small way, by giving credit to each in and through the poetry. This goes especially for all the artists, fellow writers, and professors who made possible the writing of "Austin"; notable among the number are Jim Jacobs, Dave Hickey, and three native Texas historians: Lester Gladstone Bugbee, who, before his untimely death, began work on a biography of Estevan Austin; Eugene Barker, whose subsequent *The Life of Stephen F. Austin* was indispensable; and Walter Prescott Webb, author of the classic study,

The Great Plains.

  One person important to me during my high school years, who appears in the Sabine section of "Austin," was a Methodist minister, Reverend Elwood J. Birkelbach (1917-1987). In 2016 I began a poem entitled "The Choice," something of a retrospective look at Rev. Birk, and although not properly a part of "Austin," "The Choice" is appended here for several reasons. For one thing, it adds to my memories of the minister and his having encouraged my desire to enter the ministry, and while I would decide not to do so, that decision relates to several themes in "Austin." Although "The Choice" is not directly linked to the capital city, it does allude to Austin's Colony and quotes the founder on Methodist preachers. When I began to write "The Choice," I did not have the Austin poem in mind, nor any idea of appending it to this book-length work. Thus the mention of Stephen F. Austin in "The Choice" only occurred within the context of a history of Southwestern University, one of the Methodist institutions from which Rev. Birk had graduated. (Without my realizing it at the time, my still working on "The Choice" in 2017 happened to coincide with the hundredth anniversary of the minister's birth.) If a precedent were needed for appending "The Choice" to the original Austin poem, I find one in William Carlos Williams' *Paterson*, his epic on that New Jersey city, to which he added a Book Five in 1958, seven years after the first four Books had been gathered into a single volume, and even at his death in 1963, he was working on Book Six. Williams himself observed, "I have come to understand not only that many changes have occurred in me and the world, but I have been forced to recognize that there can be no end to such a story...." My addition then of "The Choice" is ultimately a way of expanding upon one of the figures who populates the pages of "Austin" and who aids in amplifying its themes of regional history, religion, poetry, and preservation.

  From the first, I intended that after the "Proem," the Austin poem would begin with "Guadalupe," since this river street passes through the middle of the University area and therefore enabled me to follow in the epic tradition of starting "in the midst of things." From Guadalupe I would write of Sabine, the river street furthest east in the campus area, on which I first lived as a junior, after having transferred to the University from Lamar State College of Technology (now Lamar University) in Beaumont. I would then proceed west through the other six river streets: Red River, San Jacinto, San Antonio, Nueces, Rio Grande, and San Gabriel. Each street has a particular story to tell, even as all the streets, with the exception of San Antonio, relate to Estevan in one way or another. The appearance of St. Austin in "San Antonio" is a happy, coincidental reference to the saint's name given to the Catholic church and its parochial school located on that river street.

Along with the pleasure that I take in revisiting through the Austin poem its many historical figures, I also continue to enjoy the structure and the diction, rhythm, and rhyme in each of its nine sections. My plan at one point had been to shape each section into stanzas of the same number of lines as the unnumbered river-street cantos of the poem; that is, after the "Proem," which is primarily in tercets, I would write sections two through eight sequentially in couplets, tercets, quatrains, cinquains, sestets, septets, and octaves. In the process of writing, as can often happen with a poem, the river sections fell into their own stanzaic patterns, which partly spoiled my artificial scheme, and probably for the best. Even so, the different sections do involve almost all the patterns that I had envisioned. "Rio Grande" falls at times into the couplet form, and while no section is constructed of octaves, several sections are developed through a nine-line stanza, which was employed especially by Edmund Spenser, John Keats, and Lord Byron. Some sections begin in one stanza pattern and switch to another, for structural and/or thematic reasons. Obviously, none of this guarantees a successful poem, but it has been gratifying to me that I was able to work out the thoughts and themes of the different sections within or through the various stanza forms. I have always been particularly pleased with the Dantesque stanzas in the "Proem," where Estevan speaks in terzarima during his time in a Mexican jail. Perhaps a writer should not take such pride in his own work, but I confess that I have not been able to avoid doing so in the case of "Austin." Necessarily, I leave the final judgment to any reader who manages to make it through what I have long recognized to be my turgid, prolix Texas verse.

October 2017

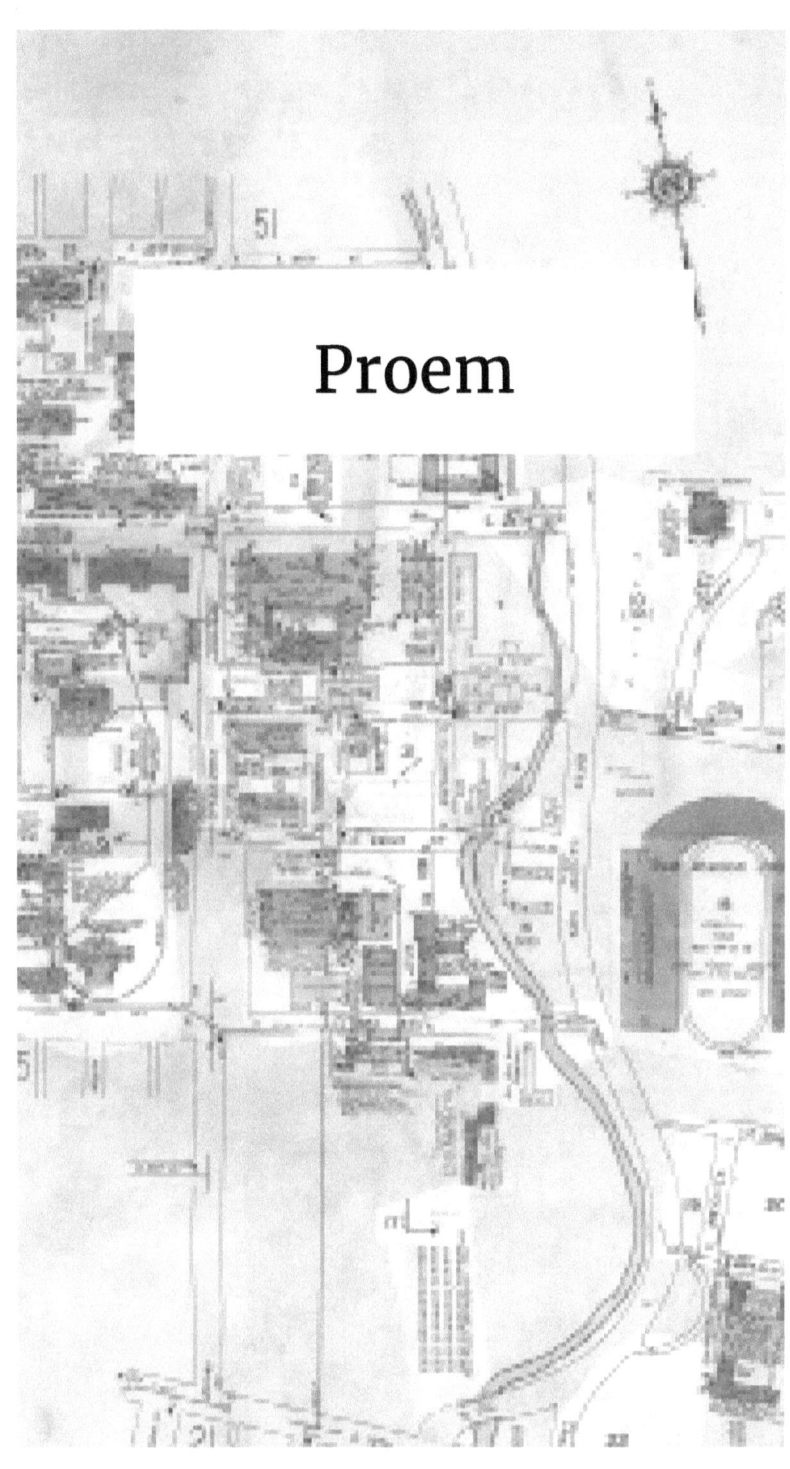

Proem

Proem

at the center   at the heart
of how & why have been & are
garden of wrongs must still recall

the seat of law & a greed feeds on
site come true from his "academy scheme"
Estevan's dream in '33

of a campus   of a where to sit & listen
at the feet of a Boatright Dobie or Webb
professors of a faith in that frontier way

vouched from a time of toughing it out
have longed somehow to touch
without a loss of here & now

their talk of cutting-horse lariat & brand
six-shooter axe & bowie-knife blade
windmill "bull wheel" cable or bit

simple tools proved so titan in hands
of men & women grown heroic-wise
in a prose of writers but rarely known

sensing none alone if not all together
may reach so deep to a meaning sought
no wildcatter logged the signs so well

could read the core & tell for certain
had come at last to salt or sand
awaiting still the drill may strike

right for singing in source or stratum
will never so soon run dry

a lease longer than for cattle or crude

may return his lay of the land
when he mapped its channels & bays
nearer his call for courses to take

in English Spanish & French
his belief in a credit line based upon
the word each man will give

at the very least to avow the debts
to summon up & render accounts
to name teachers & mates

dividends from a rented room
a class attended
memorial halls

remembered haunts
at stadium or court
the wins & losses

the leaf- & creek-veined hills
of pecan cedar & oak
have soaked like rain

have burned like sun
memory's rays now magnified
held to the page to blaze for him

who started upon the straight & error
paved the way for bones & blood
the slab laid & the cornerstone

Dave Oliphant

for every feeling & thought
for 300 yearly shining days
paid for the toll & utility bill

in his dark Inquisition cell
defrayed with the coin
of a gnawing doubt

with his visions would sire
the daily scenes
east & west on 11th Street

of Blacks still down & out
of hooker bars & liquor stores
a mere two blocks' remove

from his final resting place
his remains uprooted
from a Peach Point grave

interred in the one the State maintains
his statue in bronze by Coppini
his right & dark-green outstretched hand

extended yet toward all he hoped
would be achieved
to the ills he had not conceived

in his left a scroll unrolled
for all to read
epic of an entrepreneur

while at his back
a cape in folds

drapes to his founding feet

as he stares away
to the bier in white
the barred encased & sculpted form

of Albert Sidney Johnston
commander fell at Shiloh
directing his Rebel troops

whose ears
were it not
for that stronger stop

than the pane of glass
than the ironwork grate
would yet take in

the humble hymns
from their Shiloh Baptist choir
rise nearby & never falter

as Estevan peers to where
his indecision led
to racial slurs & bloodied fields

to where his insight failed
to where if now he looked behind
with eyes at the back of his head

he could spy across in littered yards
his slavery's kids ride metal scraps
roll tires or toss their airless balls

yelling jive in a grammar broken
as half their project homes
where just next door

his Mexican heirs
will ever insist
he stole it all

down their beers to polkas
corridos blasted out
on stereo tapes in lowered cars

in blouses loud
with red & pink
in frayed work shirts hung out to dry

swinging on plastic lines
strung from a dead mesquite
a chinaberry with its inedible fruit

the wet weight sagging them down
as lives of those
must still bear up

strive to green deep within
with a sap will flesh
the yellow seed

keep stanzas from seeing him
dragged in dirt
though each has need

of knowing earth
the bitter taste of where & when

has gotten off

deserves no greater blame
no stain
on all he tried

no tarnish on the "violet crown"
O'Henry's phrase
for this city's sunset sky

in '38 on touring 6th
& in full view
of the legislative lawns

LBJ would observe
40 families to a single lot
watched as from a single faucet

they carted water a hundred yards
one leaky tub to wash them all
an eyesore in Lyndon's House report

a crying shame so near he said
to the tallest capitol dome
its very edifice set

on a chalk named after & for
Estevan's steady ways
no shale that swells when wet

shrinks when dry
& by geologist Flawn's account
the cause of most

foundation cracks
while his own holds firm
won't shift about

to warp the floors   those at 24th
sloped where Stine Rudin & Reck
ate a meal trumpeter Michel had fixed

pasta on an old "Detroit Jewel"
his test for when
the spaghetti cooked

a gob slung
against the wall
for seeing would it stick

Estevan didn't
on that moral racial stand
waffled about unlike his stone

sold that laboring race
the real for higher stakes
though a rub can yet return

the magic gleam of all he gave
his trip to Vera Cruz
from Matamoros taking the cruise

at his own unreckoned cost
his wardrobe prairie bare
worn out long for those

stayed safe at home
yet swore he kept

prime acres for his own

no house no wife
uncaressed by an Elisabet Ney
who washed him

Ivory white
chiseled him out
in his modest suit

converted her favorite horse's hide
to a mattress stuffed
with duckling down

molding a mask
of her Artie's face
before she would burn to ash

his tender form
was never to meet
this man she made

whose hands
cold or warm
had never known

her black
inviting
shag of hair

in death his gaze still fixed upon
Johnston there below
the sleeping soldier

whose wounded frame
Elisabet's hammer turned
to a picture of painless rest

while only through Coppini eyes
the look her rival lent to him
has Estevan viewed her masterpiece

his glance as far from her own art
as his frail figure from
her Bismarck's vigorous bust

her first big break as sculptress
with Estevan only coming after
her long line of Europe's minds

a grudging Schopenhauer
agreed to a sitting
as did Grimm Garibaldi & Wagner

then made her way
through a secret wedding
on Madeira Isle

to the climate of
a Georgia farm
she hoped would cure

her consumptive lover-husband
then on with him
to Six Shooter the junction where

diphtheria carried off their little son
later to her medieval castle

her Hyde Park miniature

where Estevan came to her fingers' feel
though in his dreams she would not appear
never to lie with him in cell 15

as cold there as Johnston in repose
o what a comfort she could have been
to one ensnared by deadly men

came instead
to dress him in
a buckskin coat

its sleeves with a fashionable fringe
leaned at his side
a flintlock so admired

by crowds vacation here
stepping easily from seal to seal
of Alamo Goliad & San Jacinto

"the large hearts of heroes"
commemorated all in gold
the forced marches & firing squads

walking with ease from past to present
on the rotunda's marble floors
to gaze upon each polished plate

each governor's dates
from daguerreotype to Kodacolor
though hardly suspect

this is the man
the one with the effeminate face
so short & thin

who shouldered the load
of a warring quill
after vetoing arms year after year

writing to Mary of the carnage
of thousands slaughtered
another *Iliad* in every age

of the applause for military braid
while the unbloody pioneer
with his cause of cotton & corn

reaped no parades nor holidays
though here & there a woman won
as did Albert Sidney's wife

who sketched a picket fence
centered upon the page
on paper still unfallen

the legislature as it was in '52
in front a horse-drawn carriage
a dog behind with its tail still up

a log cabin off to the right
on top yet flying a one-star flag
his city before the Civil War

when prior to Custer's haughty fall
his wife sat down to write

of streets with armed & roaming youths

duels & feuds & rage
her words outlasting
bullets bombs & agent orange

such women might have saved the State
from its foolish ways
María too   then & now

& which of those framed here
elected to a term or two
in sessions long or short

has added even
one iota to
the law he lived

the vote his prison vision cast
for love & trust
for a fertile thought

would bring the harvest in
one these circular walls
even now retain

echoing with youthful sound
as the All-City Orchestra performs
a music Mary & Estevan should have heard

did with their own providential ears
their lives in concert then
as now these brass & winds

percussion harp & strings
among them Darío's violin
playing for a broadcast taping

while Estevan put off & shut away
no camera nor any sensitive mike
to catch him in that silent cell

yet these measures now his own
the Handel composed as if for him
these his uplifting strains

Humperdinck's his evening prayer
the pantomime of Gretel for which
each student forms the leading part

directed by Estevan's pen-baton
guided by his steadying hand
through & to a final score   a bill run up

can never settle   parents & issue ever
owing for the privilege in tune or out
for auditions won by son or daughter

their notes all meant for him
who bequeathed more than any session
has ever passed or will

than a single man can hope to leave
each generation the offspring of
his imprisonment & failing health

conferred this tall rotunda
now rings with his jottings there in jail

Austin: a Poem

made with a hidden stick of lead

thrummed his cell's Aeolian bars
with now a harmony
still reaches here

rises up & up tier after tier
to where each governor's term
needs first & last to learn his letters

each & every one by heart
to recite his thankless thirteen years
translating deeds to wilderness lands

his work with foreign words
the Spaniard's richest gift
a treasure so distrusted

still suspected as a Catholic plot
thinking the worst at its open tones
funny trills of that neighboring tongue

took from the first to be his own
spoke it to plead his Colony's case
that distant government's good

to see his colonists settled
to have them thrive
traveling there to find

as if the victim of an enchantress' spell
his six-day trip upon the Gulf
transfigured into a seasick month

in Jalapa his journey slowed again
where Perry the historian-Dean
at the end of that syndicate strike

would accept another post
had accepted the UDLA before it began
that promising permanent position

had sold the furniture & appliances for
at prices so low María swore
"You gave them all away"

then puzzled out which way to head
Albuquerque   anywhere she said
but Texas

loathed yet knew
for finding a job
the chances in this city better

loaded the VW van with cartons & plants
so piled to the roof the kids unseen
cried to leave their pet white pigeon

then limped out through a monsoon rain
the motor missing
after stopping at a Pemex station

from water had dripped into the tank
with no protective overhang
in hysterics as Darío wept & wailed

unable from within
to unlock & open

that restroom door

in Poza Rica spent a restive night
fearful attendants would break & steal
next day on to more needless worry

hearing in each sound the engine fail
so afraid would all be stranded
right in the big middle of nowhere

then made it to the Gulf's aromatic air
at Tampico the beach
& a hostel there

with its laving waves
fried redfish
& a good night's rest

then back on the road to Matamoros
passing through customs & crossing over
to a motel would take no check

to sleep upright at a roadside park
to awake worn-out & stiff   half starved
at dawn to slide the side door back

to find if the kids had ever slept
watched helplessly as her *Café de oro*
her four jars of instant coffee

rolled out & broke upon the ground
the glass & grains so quickly swept
by a puff of morning breeze

all those Mexican prospects
gone with the wind a song & film
a Bogart too but in Sierra Madre

its emptied bags of gold
mixed with sand
blown & scattered

then arrived at last in August heat
o murderous month
when tempers flare

after long hours at office desks
to stall & steam
in Mo-Pac traffic

home to stuffy air-conditioning
to plumbing in bathrooms
backing up

with cooped up kids turned into imps
tormenting the one & only mother
of this their one & only life

husband & wife
in sweltering dog-days
with their fire put out

rekindled it then
at Barton Springs
their drive renewed

by a dive into
the cool clarity of

its public pool

at Zilker Park too
with its cold solace from summer's hell
where his legacy still comes clear

nerves soothed by wading in
then recall his own nightmare
his Mexican known so well

held up by the rebel roadblock
by his passport a General
failed to endorse

as June to August had awaited too
for those papers' "final stamp"
then came by train to Distrito Federal

met by the Sullivans & rode with them
up & over mountains to that Cholula home
by the pyramid plundered by Hernán Cortés

to cobblestones of the intimate streets
in the faculty's exclusive compound
Universidad de las Américas

an Eden at the feet of snow-capped peaks
volcanic twins Iztaccihuatl & Popocatepetl
Orizaba's outline in the distance dim

came to discover had landed in the midst
of resentments ready to erupt
with a lava bed of envy & spite

he himself treated animal-like
a criminal thrown
headlong in jail

had gone as an agent
to the petty sides
then & there that very thought

caught between professors played
their losing political game
with a dictator president

flying their flags from barricades
sign of a faculty had taken control
administrators driven to Puebla

though not for long
the last word ever the purse strings'
profs armed with symbolled armbands

with academic freedom's weak demands
each campus brigade bearing the name
of some famed & martyred Marxist

instead of passing commands
from man to man
walkie-talkies

binoculars for reading
on a truck at the gate
its letters three-feet tall

"Open please, gas man"
fearful the students of engineering

might storm the chain-link fence

reliving the Revolution
in their khaki pants
he loyal

before & after
having come to serve
to assure those ran the land

his colonists all
were only afraid
of Indian raids

missed their slaves
were appealing not to be
under Coahuilan rule

& for fixing their eternal feuds
deciding their mean disputes
defending their rightful claims

of some only bought to sell
received no other recompense
than his prisoner's peso a day

used it to bribe the guard on duty
to bring him a copy
of Plato in French

said bread & water
taken with books
beat any monarch's regal meal

yet poisoned in confinement
by the lack of a diet
craved for all his days

with dialogue there reduced
to his own one-sided voice
with his cave an allegory of

his own betrayed imprisoned state
while those behind his back
worked their bag of shadowy tricks

fingers forming ferocious dogs
rattlers poised to strike
to cast aspersions

insubstantial blame
false reports
all taken back at home

as the living truth
as captive even deprived
of the light of a summer's day

his hungering mind feeding
on every glimmering fear
yet praising still

beyond the rest
those had caged him in
the Mexican

since Adam & Eve
as a work unmatched

of grand & noble design

a popular government liberal & free
with its denial of all divinity
& despotic greed

writing with passion
from his sunless cell
declared the unlettered nation

a retarded sad affair
in '32 entered his plea
to free the press

argued against those thought it best to wait
till schooling of an ignorant mass
could ready it for the printed page

esto seria lo mismo
que encerrar á uno
que tenia ojos debiles

en un cuarto enteram^{te} obscuro
sin un solo rayo de luz
con el fin de prepararle

para aguantar la luz brillante del sol—
es decir debilitar la vista mas
bajo del pretesto de fortilizarla

in his booklet
overlooked by friskers
had confiscated his few effects

registered another month & day
recording in his dim-lit dungeon
an earthquake beyond the Richter

with only a pencil to overcome
betrayal by those at home
happy to have him out of the way

those unwittingly would send to him
his violent visitation   his vision of
this city of light & learning

before its coming had felt himself
a crust of earth self-pity tore in two
his nature too quick to serve

at the beck & call
of friend & foe
had pitched him out   had locked him in

to darkness day & night
a Russia under Peter the Great
at Archangel its lone seaport

iced over half the year
"a giant closed up
in a cave with only a pinhole"

the skylight angle above
Estevan's only escape
bore him on its wings

to soar by it
through a five-hour reading space

or to contemplation before

being made once more
to breathe the lonely landscape
of its damp adobe walls

smudged by an earlier inmate
drew a serpent entwining
a Genesis tree

its crude & smutty fruit
become an image of all
he felt he had yet produced

trapped for weeks
& then let out unexpectedly
with a sentinel to guard

for an hour's walk
in the same courtyard
where in 1574

the Inquisition performed
its auto-da-fé
its public spectacle

where suddenly a flaming tree
blazed upon his sight
with its bonfire of brilliant green

& near it more dazzling still
a fountain shooting liquid sparks
so blinding to one grown overlong

accustomed only to mud & dark
now feasted on the water's fronds
leaves flashing with reflected light

crystal limbs receiving the day
then letting it fly
as birds will enter & dart away

with his mind lifted before it
as a pillar standing aglow
tall in the brightness

of its tumbling flow
a shining strength could raise
the most barren of states

nourish the roots
from head to foot
pour forth in every despair

regained his spirit
in the open air
its freshness filling his lungs

free at last from cell 15
then abruptly returned
to the serpent's den & locked back in

where tremors rocked his cot
the snake's head beginning to sway
the poisoned apples to bob

till he spoke aloud
to the venomous shades

his persecution had long aroused

What temptations can a place possess
Or is it false hope in where we go
Turns bitter the plants we long to bless?

Had it been I removed there only to know
The live oak for its grotesque shape,
Its giant shadow 'gainst summer's Vulcanic blow—

Packed in no plans the pigmy-minded ape
Can ever plumb, lugged along no dreams a small-
Ness misapprehends, held the land to no promise it ever made—

Would I lie here now an Icarus in his fall,
Brought low by those have clipped these pinions
Were spread to fly them higher? O the ingrates all!

Have let dear Sister down. What sacrifice, what privation
To follow me, and now her trust has turned to grief.
And Mary Holley's plan to bring her son,

This too heaps coals upon my head. There's no relief
For me, nor was for her in all that heat. Her trip
To Brazoria when the towboat smoked, the cabin leaked,

Her vessel moving so slowly seemed a specter ship,
Her berth as much a coffin as here this cell.
I see now the way I never shall, her slip

In the oppressive noonday sun fallen from a pale-
Ness only Horace knew, her stockings in breezeless air
Rolled from where . . . I have no right. That way lies hell,

But where else am I then? Is it not this lair
They've holed me in? Better had it been to live in sin
Than serve without a woman's love and hear them swear

That all I've done was meant for me, for Austin,
Who must be watched, suspected now of mil-
Lions hoarded, a fortune faraway in some Virgin-

Ia bank. Made in slag perhaps, had Papa stuck to lead. The wil-
Derness brought his end quicker than shot from any mine.
He returned from Bexar so fatigued, so weak and ill,

That all the blood his doctor let was drawn in vain.
That journey did him in, and now my own turns me in a single year
A misanthrope. He came to settle them all on the grant he gained,

Gone with not a thing to show, his indebtedness would never clear,
on the way back deserted by Kirkham, the powder in his gun
Wet from rain, could kill no squirrel nor deer,

Living off acorns, berries, and roots. Richmond,
His slave, exhausted the same as the horse and mule,
He abandoned down the Sabine. Philip the 2nd submitted his son

To death at the hands of the Inquisition. His religious zeal
Above and beyond paternal love. O slavery's the curse
Of curses! The robust tireless Black, his story so unreal,

Too real to hear. And mine. My Colony's slave I am, chapter and
  verse.
And how could I say of the decrepit Negro woman I own
She's not worth keeping, who's softened my clothes with harsh-

Est lye, her ladled recipes the sole feminine touch I've known.

Austin: a Poem

Have followed his deathbed wish, never to let him down.
Am so by friends on either side. My love for the Mexican

Proof to the colonists I have sold them out,
My service to him taken there as treason, to them even worse
Than murder. This government tires me now,

Have had more respect for it than it's yet deserved,
But I'm done with that. You're too impa-
Tient, he said. You want to go too fast. How not prefer

Her round full face,
Soft as an autumn moon,
Her warmth and eastern grace,

To hear and see again and soon
Her light pink lips, her open mouth,
Her hands at the keyboard or about the guitar, embracing the
    tune,

"Pensez a moi"…

& do
down every street
these thoughts of you
on walking Shoal or Waller Creek

nights relived on Hickeys' screened-in porch
at 23rd & Rio Grande
a visit spent at 24th
among those musician friends of Andy

in every garage apartment lived
on Poplar over Bracker   at San Gabriel

back of Faulkner   on Sabine above Red River
with Rudin & King   house-shoed Raja Rao on Pearl

past the littered crumbling Wooten House
with its crape myrtles
overgrown   its azaleas the city's first set out
fluted stone columns with Ionic capitals

cut by an artisan-carver "incarcerated
for drunkenness"   on the doctor's word paroled
to work on his home where alkies now recuperated
redeemed by walls & gardens DeLois restored

along the way to the best of dentists
Gerald Latimer up West 19th changed to MLK
with the snipping of his thread in Memphis
by a sniper in this nation's pay

"The Plantation of Stafford just
above Bolivar was sold
to Mr. Neal of Natches—
including 20 negroes"

through it all to find in you
a hero for this or any time
then arrive a romantic wrecked anew
by head-ons in a realist mind

yields but a one-way turn
back to that solitary confinement cell
there at least you safely earned
a right to tell your Jacksonian tale

Even before I came, Britain Baily had settled there.

Some said he had come from Kentucky, though who
Could say with Captain Brit, a character

If ever there were. The cholera in '32
Would put to rest his dubious claims. But then not all,
For he had his land, that Brazos plot, a place whereto

To breathe his last, whose walls
He'd squared and chinked, trued as best a forger could,
His wife beside him when he died. And this recalls

Not alone
What little there is to show—a bed
Shared with putting each year wed-

Lock off,
Another's sof-
Ter, fragrant arms,

Her comfort and her charms
Denied still,
Postponed, delayed until

This thankless job,
This labor has robbed
Me long, is once and for all over and done—

But how she carried out his strange request. Declared he would not
Stoop to any man, never had, was not about to in the grave.
Bid her have him buried upright, and at the bottom to put

His whisky, his rifle in his grip, to keep the coffin erect, face
It west to the setting sun, the direction journeyed
All his days. And so she did, had the hole dug just the way

Dave Oliphant

You would a well, and let him down feet first. Asserted,
Aside from never lowering himself, and the rights he swore a squat-
Ter holds to land he's come to know, title or no, a third

Claim, one wholly in line with what
I have ever held, the view that credit must reside
Not in banks but men, not in property goods or chat-

Tel slaves, but what a man has said he'll do, his pride
In how it's done, the word he gives, the stand he takes,
Never in history's chances will choose up warring sides

And trap one in between. Am caught by hate
On either hand, mistrusted, disowned by the very crowd
I am in their service to represent. It breaks

A heart like his, or makes it find in fraud
A blessedness. When word first came how in the past
Brit had been convicted, sentenced to the pen, I was proud,

Protective of my Colony's good repute, and out to see it last,
So ordered Baily gone, decamped within three days, or else.
Replied that yes he'd served, behind the bars, but too by cast-

Ing votes. Had held elective office in the Commonwealth,
Opposing there the rabbit-like increase of a Monster Bank. Took
The Law upon himself, tempted on a smaller scale

To do as the Second on a grander did. Turned a petty crook,
Fabricated bills, interest free, then paid in full.
Let out, he stole away to this godforsaken place, where it looked

To him he'd at last be left alone, not called upon to pull
Another's load. Had his crime behind, his solitary life ahead.

Austin: a Poem

On hearing this, ready to believe, yet not to be a gull,

I rode to visit Brit, listened in delight to all he said,
Saw his farm progressing right along, left him there
To find his peace, and know he did. Dead and buried

Is better off. Can see how our ways compare,
His hopes for keeping friends from wrack and ruin,
Usurious rates. In remembrance seem to wear

His very shoes, pinched by those I warned against
The agents sold them land on scrip, counterfeit
As Baily's bills, though none of those so innocent.

& on hearing you now have come again
to follow down each hall each river street
intent on recovering those lives from then
through an account though it's incomplete

will trace those still most vivid & reinvest
in all you intended this place should mean
revealed through friends & those professed
their ways in words these lines would glean

Guadalupe

Guadalupe

begin *in medias res*
with this artery named
for a town in New Spain took its own
from another left behind
by conquistadors set their billowing sails
to rejuvenate the old through endless veins
ingots up the Indian anus   sneaked out
from royal shafts   brought to piles
down from mystic pyramids

was where her temple stood
protectoress of
the Totonacs
Tonantzin she
mild goddess of
their earth & corn
not human blood
but turtledoves
birds she bid them bring

even there where later
the Mother of God would come
to a native of Cuatitlan
his Nahuatl appellation
changed to Juan
at her command gathered roses from
a barren hill of Tepeyac
with stars imprinted about her image
on a dark-blue maguey cloth

is here a thoroughfare to drive or walk
awake or in remembered dreams
by night in its azure light
by day beneath its cerulean skies

far from his vision in that humid cell
her miracle hung from hut to cathedral
a guide for taxi or transit bus
Virgin still is giving birth
to the hopes of rich & poor

this street bears her name's sensual sound
though one so mispronounced
or call it "The Drag" instead
to some perhaps   to others none
each corner to the latter an angle on
measures more than surveys made
to those can look & slowly gauge
where & when each picture show
each window & glass door opened

yet closed to those
with darker skins
could never enter to see a film
even Indian friends
would file then back & forth
with signs to let them in
cursed by the weekend crowds
cordoned by ushers heard the repeated phrase
"Do you sell tickets to every color & race?"

its pavement gave & still gives now
welcome to the wandering mind
the hero home to wife & child
the wastrel's return from exotic points
to where it all began & comes back true
a dream of renewal within the old
within the steady stream of those
once gathered & started here

a parade rejoined & marching to

incarnations one & all
of more than they could even know
beyond their own unspoken prayers
any hopes had dared to hold
kept secret from a deepest need
yet in getting ahead driven off the course
left high & dry by the push to arrive
till now at last to have their say
to find it even in this narrow way

would bring them back
to this city signed their lease
the one they had to break
to tack in search of freedom's fleece
karats of computers & seismographs
only too late to discover it flat
had fallen from that earlier grace
a disillusioned crew blown here again
restored by this Aeolus memory bag

recounts those days on rented skates
wheelchairs run on rechargeable cells
a shuttle bicycle moped or roller board
blind with dogs or tapped white sticks
a short brawny guy clicked his tongue
as a sonar sound bounced off the curb
would tell him when & where to step
for making his way along this street
better than any assumed so self-assured

before their truest path abandoned
misled by a salary a degree held out

only in leaving it to learn the truth
or stopped by Charlie's deadly aim
in a close-up of that tragic scene
the bloody part Fred Eckman's son
acted in a play of Greek invention
wherein the mortal flesh & blood
brought home its distant meaning

now step back in to that current again
a plugging of lives back into then
a Herakleitian change unstops the ears
on retaking Eckman's Whitman class
once more his marriage upon the rocks
Scylla & Charybdis to Odysseus' ship
steering in '60 down this river street
a ligustrum sprig between thumb & finger
in place of lilacs in Walt's elegiac lines

taught in Fred's course on *Leaves of Grass*
would set this too   though only later
after being lured east by WCW's contagious writing
on green glass shards & the hospital road in spring
before returning at last to the one known here
the State's Lunatic Asylum past 38th
where can still take in its 1873 idyll
Edward King's "live oaks near at hand"
more "a temple" than a "retreat of clouded reason"

made to see it first through Michael Evans'
"Mother Had Dementia Praecox Too"
printed in '63 in *Triad* issue number 2
"The hospital. I'd seen it,
the old stone buildings crawling
with ivy, the vacant-eyed patients

spitting out between the bars
at passersby; . . . you're a rebel
fighting something that's unfightable

. . . and that twisted poetry you write
. . . it's for your own good . . .
. . . The iron doors . . . closed behind. . . ."
later by a call one night from a man inside
committed by those feared all he knew
said his tale could make a mint
just bring a lawyer & a tape recorder
would reveal how high up the corruption went
of that part of his story never in doubt

said type it up   sell it to the media
they'll pay you at the highest asking price
as for him release would be his only take
insisted   then made it please   then pleaded
to save him from the others would not believe
it was all a mistake   he wasn't one of them
heard those trying to cut him off   to break in
get back away from here he began to shout
& after that the line went dead

cattycorner a flower vendor living under a bridge
would serenade bus loads with his cornet tunes
the Stinky Lady wore urine-stained polyester pants
Bicycle Annie of alpine pack & aluminum crutch
smashed a driver's watch crystal for helping lift
one of her secret-filled bags & her plastic sack
a frantic rider miles from where he'd gotten on
missed his winter jacket left on a Capitol bench
felt its warm sleeves entered by another's arms

Caveman slept under cliffs beside Shoal Creek
eater of trash & in five years never once sick
would pick it up too to keep this street litter-free
in front of St. Austin's offered scavenged bottles
unopened vodka a quart of rosé a crème de menthe
in garbage bin even came across a Bollingen Plato
claimed he had read all the hundred great books
said Ariosto's *Orlando Furioso* his favorite epic
recommended love's lost tears in moon-travel canto

boat people had survived & worked their way
to its far reaches three winding blocks north of
Irma Drive at Airport where that friendly Thai
opened & named his grocery Oriental Market
its shelves & aisles heavy with a seaweed smell
burned perhaps by some rival from years before
rebuilt & became the neighborhood's only store
for buying Anytime or orange Commuter cards
never bothered on checks to take down the TDL

El Toro at 16th where Hickey had wolfed down
almost inhaled its enchiladas with cheese & chili
his description in *Riata* of those buttered tortillas
even now the mouth waters at his chosen words
& with Beeson had lived off their refried beans
George would say "hot plate" before waiter could
when he would come to serve the towel-held order
tickled to catch the look on his brown-skinned face
so surprised so upstaged by his own simple phrase

even María came to try one of their enchilada plates
& though a resident alien who for at least five years
grew ill from the lard & corn reek in any such meal
allowed it not half bad & cooks in its Tex-Mex style

yet still can't stand the questions perennial as weeds
"What kind of Mexican food do you eat in Chile?"
"What do you have there for Thanksgiving dinner?"
when from her lovely lips comes a debater's reply
"The Mayflower never made it south of the border"

back of the Nighthawk from his room on Whitis
George would go at 3 a.m. for a size-royal snack
Jim for orange juice freshly squeezed & half a stack
next door to the florist for *Riata*'s grosgrain ribbon
with Morton or Jon passed it from the public library
with a recording of Ives' bases-loaded piano sonata
another pilgrimage taken with that solemn vow
to be fulfilled on recalling the façades & faces
as a shrine to Estevan & to his going without

at Dacy's Campus Shoes in display windows
those penny loafers sold in '65 so all the rage
with their leather lips caressing shiny coppers
bright coins of dress-alike sorority sisters
from there to Chile whose mines remain
the veins of a people still drained to pay
for bargains on sale in that Lebanese store
heard it sung in protest in cold Santiago
fitting their sexy feet in homesick dreams

chaste & chastening nights yet unexpired
as his darkened days still bring to light
visions seen then & glimpsed again
in the flood of those go flashing by
swept up in the undertow of this river street
reborn on its miracles both new & old
by a Mexican town remembered Spain's
all blended roiled within & interfused

to render forever the homage he's due

who bought the future at his own expense
fortunes of few amassed from his making do
in return to sing the Co-op's "cattle crossing"
to revisit Elisa's Reilly Elementary School
leather-lunged evangelist & Viet eggroll stand
all the streets in a row as they ripple & weave
from east to west in their order within his state
as each too from the Sabine to the Rio Grande
flows through this city bears his proper name

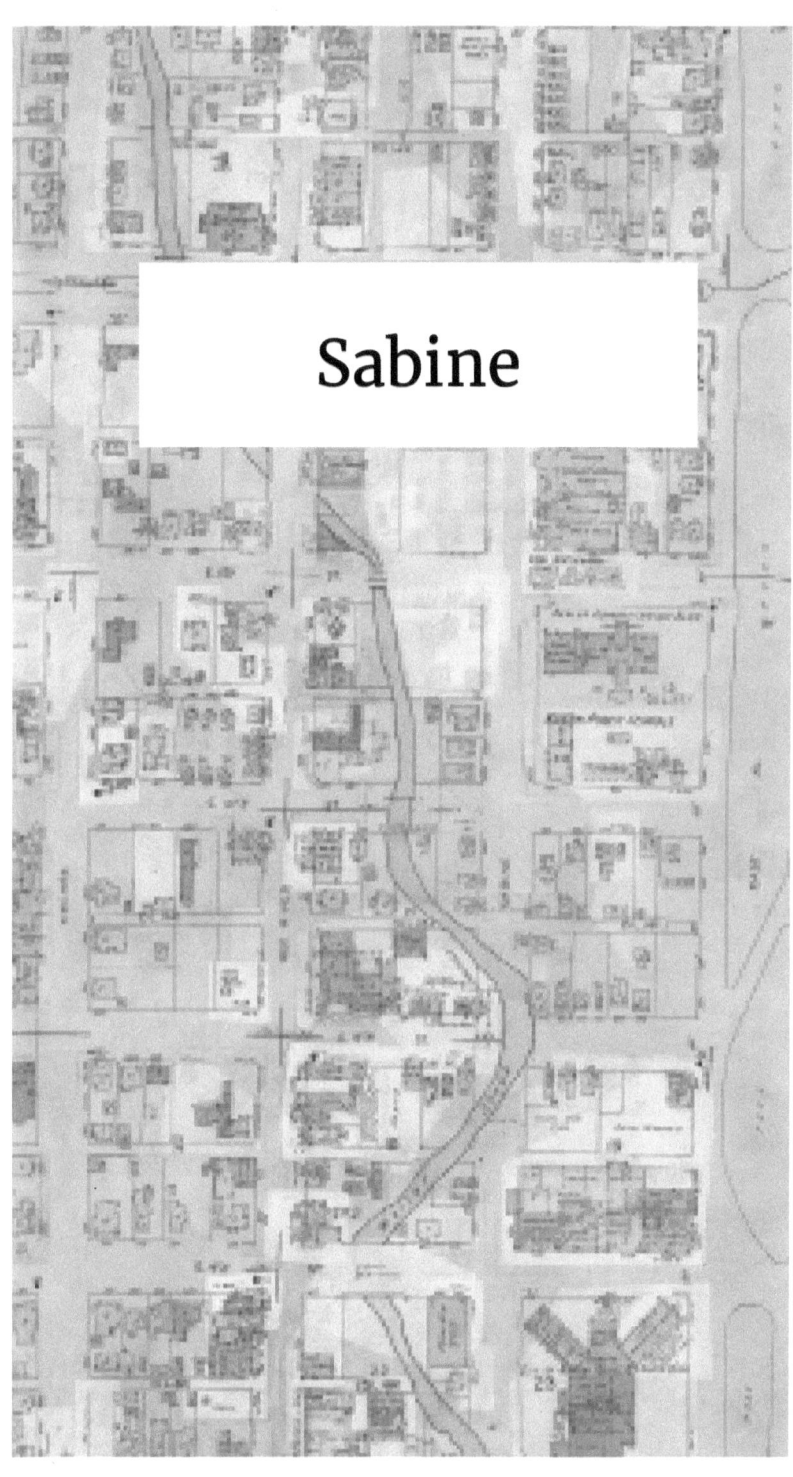

Sabine

Sabine

      that first semester here & as it should began
      on this street furthest east in Waller's plan
      where Andy had picked out the fanciest pad
      shared with Gordon who ducked out early
      for the old Music Building's recital hall
      to practice on the organ reserved for then
      or so he'd claim when his turn had come
      to do the dishes   huge feet (*patudo* in Chile)
      a mystery how he played one pedal at a time

      but was needed to meet that higher rent
      with the apartment too expensive for two
      though Andy offered to pay the difference
      unable then to believe the invasion at night
      when a sudden flash lit its one long room
      as he screamed & leaped straight up in bed
      so certain was struck by a lightning bolt
      then said he awakened & suddenly felt
      a giant rat sitting right on his chest

      unaffected by little traps set out for them
      they would saunter off after eating the cheese
      with a broom beat them off the garbage sacks
      called the landlord said Just pinch their necks
      later on to bring over his steel-toothed claws
      to catch them coming out through every hole
      in that luxury apartment's limestone walls
      would not have had them with cheaper rates
      yet remembered more for that promise made

      after seeing an e.e. imitation in a display case
      Bass's "o orange water lily" had won 1st place
      in reaction the urge born to respond one day
      how another's prize was to open the way

from that hall in Parlin to her Chilean face
& in '79 to follow in his steps at the HRC
working as James Bagg's editorial assistant
being saved from selling shoes with a Ph.D.
starts given by Bob's win & the job he quit

his poem from *Corral* in that hallway exhibit
across from one with Eckman's double sonnet
both outside of Mody Boatright's office door
Chairman of English who then had shuffled in
to that class was taking on the Age of Darwin
ash from his stogie flaking up & falling away
or chewed too short & soggy to light it again
his lecture on Hawthorne's prairie conflagration
indelible as a fire-resistant Bible's asbestos say

another on social evolution of Wm. Graham Sumner
who viewed struggle for survival a condition of man
poverty not to be abolished by the passing of laws
but by working each day that the weak grow strong
typed a term paper on Progress at that kitchen bar
while nightly overhead Neanderthals rolled
a cave-entrance rock or a giant mixing bowl
another mystery now segues from this river street
to its namesake when a freshman attending Lamar

crossed it with Burkart's Brass Ensemble
for a performance in Baton Rouge at LSU
of that joyous piece Paul Holmes composed
in '58 in Beaumont he Abilene-born in '23
studied theory here in the old music rooms
just a stone's throw away from Guadalupe
his pock-marked face   hands extra-large
a man of gangly build & of a sallow skin

his notes ever vibrant so warm & clear

such care he took to copy them out
each player's part in manuscript
with stems & rests a match in ink
for his sound so infectious so elegant
conveyed by his every ringing phrase
& his penmanship would even seem
to make the tricky upbeat rhythms
the sudden acrobatic leaps
all somehow to come out right

the shock of discord never his way
reason enough his work is rarely heard
would admit he liked Hindemith a bit
mostly fugues & sarabandes of J.S. Bach
but listened little to fellow composers
fearing to drown in the influence pool
Andy considered it sinking not to swim
both then standing as guardian angels
each whispering a differing what to do

would hear the others & hear them still
any hope this poem may stay afloat
so dependent on each & every one
as much on Estevan's life & letters
for a launching again where & when
those student friends had rented then
theirs the hows & whys of many a line
would lift now their voices & lives
in a writing meant to keep them current

Holmes who wrote for harmony more
than for any thought of fame or glory

& the same holds true for Estevan too
as when in '26 with things still touch & go
he sent his warning to both bickering sides
to swallow pride & lay their arms aside
addressed his hard but friendly epistles
to a self-styled commandant had just as he
after tedious waiting won a grant to settle

pero nada que ver con él
Edwards whose impudence had led to
outpouring & clamor of public protest
from those had long before he came
found a spot with its greater promise
who forded their wives & kids & hogs
across this stream   the same Sabine
would name this redivivus river street
later the Louisiana-Texas dividing line

near Nacogdoches along this side
with its banks forever shaded by
dogwood sweetgum red & white pine
announced he'd send them back again
have every squatter bound in chains
his threats he bragged a hurricane
the Spaniards he branded an idle lot
stirred the Indians to join his band
for running those "foreigners" off

bribed their chieftains Mush & Bowl
declared their sacred burial grounds
a Republic of free men born to reign
shouted down the Mexican government
till then he & followers forced to flee
sent packing by their own red flags

their rhetoric of a thundering storm
hightailed it across that very stream
as Estevan tamed such typhoon talk

with his words to the listening ear
no truer music will one ever hear
concord recalled by a river's street
its name recording a time & place
when tempers ran a raging tempest
a floodwater of cacophonous cries
a drowning out of all common sense
till calmed by the warm clear tones
of Estevan's admonishing prose

in turn reminds of that composer's notes
Holmes' "Lento for Tuba and Piano"
a piece inspired by Robert LeBlanc
student switched from a lucrative career
as chemical or petroleum engineer
to that instrument awkward & slow
though with diaphragm under control
could hold his breath then boom it out
to pump to life Paul's song & dance

as Estevan too had held it in
his counsel kept but then released
in measured phrases render still
his advice so sound & soothing

"I would write directly
to the Governor of the State
Give him a full statement of facts
and a very minute history of the acts

Write in *English* and make an apology
for doing so   It is perhaps
a fortunate thing I have learned patience
in the hard School of an Empresario

for I assure you
that in this place
I have had full use
of all I possessed

Gaines and a few others
blamed Ahumada and me
for the course I advised
Fields and Hunter

are certainly killed
by the Cherokees
and all the other leaders
of his fanatic party

have escaped across the Sabine
and I advised a mild course
with those who were compromitted
in a secondary degree

Ahumada chose to pursue it
and for this a few blame me
but I have a consolation
worth more than the approbation of any

and the Mexican character stands higher now
than it ever did before   I hope the people of the Colony
will be satisfied for *theirs* is worth more to me
than all the world besides"

his words remembered through Holmes
whose very music evokes Estevan
forgotten there in his distant cell

in '22 had first come over
in dark as to his *Lively*'s fate
having left before he even knew

the company & its cargo landed safe
feared those aboard that ship
which he had bought

with seeds provisions & implements
all were lost
gone down in a coastal squall

had come ahead to secure for them
a place to settle
to lay a claim to lands for those

might never see the shore again
nor speak Spain's unfriendly tongue
nor even their own

seventeen there were
& Lovelace one
who loaned him toward the *Lively*'s cost

came not knowing what Fortune would hold
in '56 a century later & even more
would come to meet the Governor

in uniform here to represent
the Council's Neches troops

Austin: a Poem

another river lived along

the photo still retain
taken then at the shaking of
Allan Shivers' hand

wearing that brown Explorer tie
with Eagle badge & Beaumont sign
a print shows adolescent shining eyes

though could not foresee the how nor why
of a whole life plotted here
as if Estevan had mapped it out

fallen upon by a Comanche band
took the little he had
then gave it back

all but the blankets
his bridle & mainly
his Spanish grammar

crossed the Medina into
the poorest land
he had ever seen

a country vacant of everything
but prickly pear   to him Laredo the site
of perpetual drought & indolence

then traveled on from there
never once inspired
nor Humboldt either not long before

who hoped no other spot on earth
could prove so miserable as what he saw
between Monterrey & Mexico

a judgment shared too by Berlandier
"a lover of solitude
and of picturesque views"

who found its "small groves
of huisache
—whose hairy fruits

make ink as good as gall—
the only ones which even slightly
interrupt the area's monotony"

had encountered no herbaceous plants
but then the Frenchman notes
"despite the apparent barrenness

numerous herds graze nourished by
the thorny nopal . . .
a wagon wheel broken on our first day out"

in '76 traveling there by car
could not compare
for protected by tires from amygdaloids

earlier in '60 had come to play
a wayward erratic part
in Estevan's grandest scheme

his "seminary of learning"
though undreamed of in '56

dressed in that suit of forest green

a poor excuse for an Explorer Scout
planning then to minister
to pursue the course prescribed

by Reverend Elwood Birkelbach
whose own began
at Jones Prairie & Walker's Creek

with boyhood idols of Buffalo Bill
& a threatened Texas Ranger
had hidden in the tall thick chaparral

drafted as chaplain to an island where
"The Purple Shaft" would plow into
the planes parked & loaded there

164 dead from 10 explosions
his own skull torn
when oxygen tanks

blew a concussion meant would ever after
on administering Communion to his congregants
stop & stuff Kleenexes up his nose

done he said out of all respect
or would drip bright red
on the silver plate

this at St. Paul's
Beaumont's South Park Methodist church
where would suffer then a breakdown

when sent by the Synod to recover
at a smaller appointment in Rusk
with its famous hospital

handy just in case
serving there his fewer souls
yet could still forget his flock

as his mind sped onward
to a scene envisioned
at a frontier fort

its noonday sun glaring down upon
a dry parade ground from out of the past
inside its stockade a change of guard

when on the tip of an officer's sword
would flash the blinding eye of the Lord
contained & connected all time & space

wanted so to read as he   omnivorously
though too lazy ever to keep the pace
of his devouring one author's volumes

before taking up another's
had said should attend Lon Morris first
then Southwestern above the San Gabriel's banks

his alma mater oldest university in State
had heard like him that inner call
for a man of the cloth

or had thought then intended to be
though later recalled

at evening worship

the sermon he delivered upon
a farmer stumbled behind his mule
when up in the sky

spied a big PC
took it as a sign to go Preach Christ
laid down his reins & answered

yet after years of riding circuit
decided to Plow Corn
was all it had meant

came likewise instead
to this river street
where a first Poem Cast

here where Barker begins Estevan's trip
never to enter as Birk advised
the Perkins Seminary at SMU

nor to know back then Estevan's vision
the trail Moses blazed so overgrown
with belief had already passed beyond

any silly high school history course
one so filled with useless dates
the fiery cloud still up ahead

of the pillars had gone before
those would lend instruction in
a poetry struck from desert stone

though even Estevan missed the way
such lines may follow
from Berlandier's road to Monterrey

where huisache made
the writing flow
& now with this backwards glance

retrace that route once more
with its each wrong turn
would come out right

drove the Volks from Ciudad Victoria
through mountains seemed unending
the engine straining up one side

breaks whining down the other
around the winding curves
where grinding trucks

hogged those narrow roads
from them to view from far above
each lush precipitous inviting plunge

each range revealing a higher yet
till reached at last that valley floor
its cacti on which the Aztecs saw

their prophecy's wriggling snake
caught in an eagle's beak
& in spite of all as it did for him

that trying year of highs & lows
a benefaction still endures

his own to most may never know

nor ever care how much they owe
beyond any estimate or budget spent
with his limited funds then running dry

had sold his watch for food & drink
for posting the latest news to his brother Jim
drawing on Hawkins to tide him over

then ran into that Englishman
would loan him a little more
a General on a mission for

the very Republic of Chile
had fought against a Spanish rule
an ambassador who

perked up at Estevan's Texas plan
even agreed to split with him
any grant should come his way

& just the same would Wavell
share whatever lands the Texan gained
Arthur Goodall

a guide well-versed in Latin life
his Spanish good
Estevan's improving day by day

wrote to the Congress as best he could
appealed they stay decentralized
not to keep as the Romans had

every province bound to Rome
not to make of its capital city
the nation's single seat & center

then Wavell on reminiscing
told of the audacious attack Lord Cochrane led
his capture of Valdivia's fortress

at that southern port to which Cortínez extended
an invitation to talk on Spain & Wm. Carlos Williams
in a Spanish even now no match for Estevan's own

there to meet Carlos' dancer wife   later estranged
& Omar Lara his poet-communist friend
exiled in Rumania after Allende's fall

as was Gonzalo Millán in Montreal
& Oscar Hahn of black rose fame
who had come to this State in '62

he too a part of the same
Chile-Texas exchange
had in turn gone there in '65

returning alone in '66
with María & Darío in '71
Hahn's generation read & followed

translated their lines & lives
those as vines & tendrils kept curling back
to their long thin envisioned land

a tree whose limbs
they would lop but loved

as Hahn who in '73

fled to a salaried job
in Maryland & later in the Iowa Workshop
before that Oscar taught in Arica when

his colleagues would all give welcome
when lectured in that very same room
where shortly before Vargas Llosa had come

to deliver they said his magisterial speech
though Oscar not to appear
greet hear or be seen with

a Texan spoke so haltingly
then Ramón Layera to end up here
with Jo & their kids exposed

to his trial by fire for tenure
rendering Harryette Mullen for Prickly Pear
before that had brought over Lawrence Benford

in Arica led by Ramón & Espagne Pauner
calmly through those thorny fields
of fists & objections the leftists raised

escorted too by Alicia & Oliver
being excused on his radio show
for imperfect tense & faulty case

yet there by chance to use
a Chilean expression so dear to all
"to think oneself the death in boat"

got a laugh from their comic phrase
then how many later herded aboard
sailed off to years of wistfulness

the disillusion in letters Oliver wrote
from the Party's promises unfulfilled
he & Alicia never playing the part

the convenient role of refugees
from quote the C.I.A.'s overthrow
took their lumps in Birmingham

struggled through without complaint
in '71 a turn of events so unforeseen
though in '66 Carlos looked even then

to leave Valdivia's endless rain
its only other season/station the one for trains
its earth damp three hundred sixty-five days

where humid clothing hung to dry
before the oil or paraffin stove
smoked until the windows fogged

his books of Borges' poems
known from then
a friendship formed of all these years

begun from where
Lord Cochrane & his men had climbed
through cannon fire from high above

working their way through mud & timber
up paths along the sheer rock cliffs

Carlos himself later under the gun

on leaving behind wife & children
coming to scale in Iowan drifts
steep bulwarks of a PhD

to storm his way to victory
to win it in himself
the going tough

bogged down by dull demands
delayed by deep affections
pinned him down

the daily need for love
escaped by none
most when far from home

the assault on a foreign front
an endless siege
then came to share

to walk this city's river streets
as had with him where Cochrane won
his visit here a dream come true

showing him Estevan's setting for
his longed-for language school
& what did he feel

when Wavell spoke
of Carlos'
Andean land

did he see his Colony gazing south
creating bonds as close as these
turning from a deep dependence on

the east with its hold like Rome's
know common views could bridge the gulf
establish a Mediterranean trade & art

on recalling his talk with that British man
now climb once more
Cerro Santa Lucía

at the center   at the heart
of María's capital city
her country too

there where Pedro de Valdivia
battled the Araucano in epic form
there where Santiago founded

on eucalyptus-shaded lovers' hill
with its statue of Caupolicán
his bow drawn

his war ending for him
as he sat upon
the Spaniard's sharpened pole

broke & gored his innards
with pain enough
to weep & plead

yet met his death without grimace
his face serene

his eyebrows untwitching

in ecstasy as though
on their wedding bed
until at his feet Fresia to throw

their son who suckled her breasts
child of a captive father
had changed his sex

severed in shame their sacred knot
Ercilla's history from María's lips
tasted ever after with each caress

carried there to find & hold her fast
by this river street goes through no more
by an apartment then so overpriced

gone down before
the wrecking ball
of campus expansion

two cities
two continents
spliced as one

by a minor composer's major chords
by a tuning to
an impresario's fervent prose

links from Apennines to Andes
farms since Horace a plantation near Bolivar
at St. Paul's a minister spread the gospel

his good word pointing the road to read
irked by a poem & stirred to reply
though none would ever quite satisfy

yet from that beginning
the endless apprenticeship
& in '65 to be selected

as one of fifteen student leaders
among them Ricardo Romo
track-star-historian

then the finding María there
librarian at the binational center
she the more than hoped-for answer

to a life together
on tying her Chilean
with Texan strands

no Wm. Graham Sumner's
loose connection
but a Explorer's bowline scripture

would never unravel
knot in a tangle
not ever slip

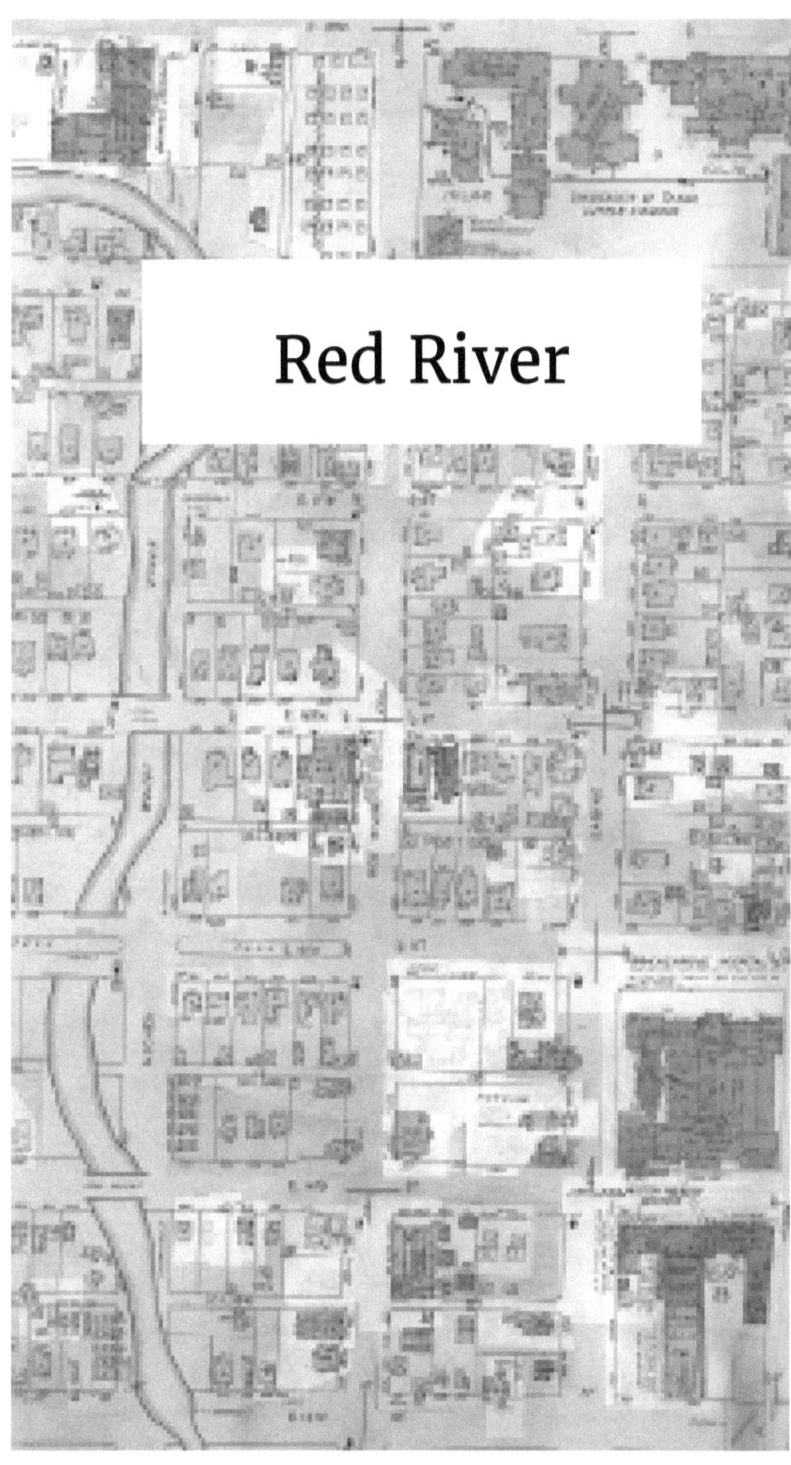

Red River

Austin: a Poem

Red River

with its sandy land & ruddy undrinkable water
Altus a Texas town till they switched the border
from north to prairie dog of this river's forks
on either side salt cedars wheat & sorghum
yet to live on the other what a difference it made
caught sore throats from breathing its dusty air
longed each day for home & a place would swear
grew crops superior to those an Okie could grow
picked up & espoused ever after views so narrow

would make an exception of that Sooner hound
unable to forget or deny Cubby's knowing look
his name mother chose when she volunteered
to take on that rambunctious Cub Scout den
he a part rat terrier wore each badge in turn
sewn on a leather patch hung from his collar
Wolf Lion Webelo (no Bear with a change of age)
for hikes would wrap in wax-paper his half-a-can
swam the Neches twice more than earned an Eagle

survived Houston to whimper under a Beaumont bed
buried by Hildebrandt Bayou he loved the best
a slough out near the Humble refinery camp
where he had chased & barked & dug in holes
after brown swamp rabbits & the armadillos
slowly lost his hearing then hit by a car
crawled home to music room behind garage
far from his birthplace where in alien fields
locusts on mesquites sing & shed their shells

with Mom Dad & brother Tom to return
back across the south fork of this river line
to stay with Granny that first summer there
a week in Fort Worth to cure whatever ailed

has ever been the same outside of this State
in Mexico once more an illness took its toll
while María happy to speak her *lengua* again
to barter in the shops & the open-air stalls
was laid up for days from just the smells

as Estevan languished in that dingy cell
feverish with dreams of live oak & pecan
with fears his colonists would overreact
saw Butler with horns & a pointed tail
misguiding them all to dissension & war
uncertain if his letters delivered or read
his patience tried if not beyond about as far
as the trials Ben Franklin or a Job endured
his prayer one last time to see Peach Point

to be with Mary & sit silent in the shade
of the sweetgum formed a canopy above
in a blend of holly & her sun-dried hair
their thoughts entwining as covering from
the political sun with its nightmare rays
to make it back home & the work to be done
to bring them together & better each one
or forget them & think of himself for a change
o best to recall the snail & its lowly pace

have a local mind from that inextricable time
uprooted at nine by Dad's decision to move
to cross over & sell his Great American Life
to farmers would teach the pulling of bolls
to drive the muddy roads & hook blue cat
bass with mouths could open big as a fist
then back across to visit with Alvin & Sis
reading on the way of Tom & Huck in a cave

but from any moving car grew nauseous sick

never to make it through those classic books
for a dozen years or maybe was even more
for sure not here in '60 that spring semester
read instead Dickens' *Great Expectations*
Gogol Dostoyevsky & some Latin to boot
sharing then that rat-infested luxurious flat
on Sabine one block east of this river street
where first David Reck & Jon Bracker later
set down in rented rooms their notes or poems

at repainted desks one creating a 12-tone piece
the other his lines on Scholz's bier Garten song
those houses now asphalt seas & live-oak isles
lost for the sake of late models parked on tar
on weekends for the Longhorns' fanatical fans
chanting as defenses shut down Hogs or Frogs
rarely missed Mustang Bear or Cougar contests
now want them back as a signal caller's errant pass
as on 'Horns' last possession linebacker intercepts

antique elms removed at Frank Erwin's orders
defiant students chaining themselves to those
despising that Regents Chair with half-lens frames
was he too who killed the Chile-Texas Exchange
Dean Bob King surprised to learn opera his passion
Ron Seeliger mastered Italian listening to the Met
for six Saturdays a year sacked summer's relief
from May to October the protective green leaves
admit with higher rises number of seats increased

for viewing artificial yards in a conference race
with Wally Pryor summing up the play by play

that feeling of a saving tackle a handoff taken
of gaining the first & ten on a third down five
or on a quick-opener to pop through & break it
not turn the ball over on a final critical drive
sucking it up for a last-ditch come-from-behind
snag a sideline toss & tight-walk still in bounds
dancing into the end zone as clock runs down

same as Joseph Jones of Waller Creek fame
need trees & plants yet also athletic lessons
a way for Darío to earn some pocket change
by selling in stands his sodas to thirsty fans
for their fraternity flasks of instant courage
as after practicing etudes & Bach partitas
after exercises in math & in chemistry lab
he would await his turn at the back of the line
for the trays of Cokes toted to blasting bands

at half-time their marches to intricate patterns
those formed on the field while staying in step
to memorized tunes practiced morning & night
forming letters & emblems & human designs
performing as they kept each other in mind
all as one to execute their sharp to the rears
pivoting for a diagonal on precisely the spot
re-rehearsing routines & if put down as dull
held up an end belonged had a weight to pull

later on would prefer Rice's chaotic "Mob"
its disorderly helter-skelter in non-uniforms
darting any which way to avoid a semblance
then came together to spell their rival's name
to pay tribute playing an opposing fight song
to the applause for making such fun of it all

yet included too a social or a political point
a current comment on a world gone wrong
as crowds consumed nachos & salty popcorn

Estevan's city for memories not these alone
destined as well for the others soon to come
to rent at "The Overlook" odious condominium
erected by "The Shiflet Group" ruined the view
from windows where in July's sweltering heat
could observe the cool bamboo on Poplar Street
one block long yet never remembered as short
in thought from semesters there going on & on
unlike a student account stamped overdrawn

on demand each matching garage apartment
pays the bearer in full from a formative day
with its arch at the foot of a wooden stairway
a set ascending the inner walls of all who are
fruitful though facing any bare treeless yard
still stuccoed white from that unrushed time
when few owned much less could afford a car
walking to classes & for the week's supplies
to Paramount sneak previews Sunday nights

Peyton Place or *Blood and* (wilted) *Roses*
then back to campus through Capitol dome
by way of Elisabet Ney's the leading man
though his coming attractions untaken in
with history never seeming as real as film
girl's first kiss vampire's teeth at her throat
set hearts throbbing not agrarian thoughts
his lines from a letter dated Brasoria 1829
on nothing more than the crop brought in

on Poplar would meet Bracker by accident
in his rented room below & behind garage
a package for him left in that upstairs box
on taking it down had knocked at his door
to be welcomed in to the rest of his life
to his heating plate & his green potatoes
his painting by Klapp of people eating
to long talks with him of Keats & Yeats
listening to opera Mozart & Beethoven

in Amarillo would begin his *Penny Poems*
his cards & letters later arrived from Paris
Terre Haute New York or Slippery Rock
San Francisco Hawaii Manila Singapore
in Japan a towering giant ever ill at ease
with his prominent feet & outsized nose
wandered at sea with his extra baggage
of a sister unvisited a mother unwritten
heavy load of a wife he had given up on

would stop by at times but never to tarry
planned once more to start fresh & settle
his poems moving in spite of constraints
to make them pleasant by whatever rules
had painted there the portrait of his father
left it with somebody or other somewhere
made sketches scattered as so many leaves
in '61 had sat for him there in his only chair
then grew morose & withdrew from school

had all come after falling out with George
& once he had left had roomed there alone
when Jon a boon yet everywhere injustice
in despair headed back home to Beaumont

then in June would return & try it again
renting with Andy that other twin side
the eastern upstairs with Lloyd below
hefty student joked of his being blind
spent his tuition on a trip to the coast

those carefree days when parents paid
for the learning more outside of classes
than from all those were required to take
appalled by failures & switching of majors
living in rooms looked to them like pig sties
dirty clothes under beds or thrown in closets
weeks of unwashed dishes so fungus-caked
so anguished to understand the finding fault
with truths they acquired much harder ways

in '28 Andy's own folks Margaret & Paul
students then at nearby Texas Wesleyan
its director Reverend Olander Swedish too
in its college co-op both earning their keep
by doing such chores as milking the cows
their fees by cleaning the dormitory house
their teachers themselves students at U of T
where later they attended & pursued degrees
till quit with Depression to make ends meet

she a maiden Anderson from over by Manor
August her father had styled himself an author
stole time from breadwinning to finish his text
written in his lively & readable patriotic prose
proud to be a *Hyphenated* man as Swenson too
an immigrant citizen tied to his newfound land
& also Sir Swante Palm that collector of books
by those like Charles Darwin considered kooks

neighbors howled when August printed his own

Paul too a second generation but born near Hutto
a little crossing on the wet fork of the San Gabriel
rose three miles wide moved a plumbingless house
his blacksmith father told the story & "as it goes
when none could settle on a name for the town
one Swede had spoken up 'guess we gotta Jonah'
and it stuck"   also regaled with slow endless tales
of putting in a sulfur plant in a Wyoming snowstorm
"well now you might say it weren't exactly no snap"

nor was it then to explain to a friend
or write a poem meant what was meant
much less find the girl would last forever
ask Andy who thought for certain he did
a redhead from Lamesa had led him on
& how many would feel it wasn't worth it
when always the words just came out wrong
in Batts Hall inspired by the native speakers
on exams their accents made no sense at all

in Latin had James Hitt & Christian Smith
have never gotten over having ever let go
of that dead language they offered alive
after convoluted Cicero had then arrived
at *The Aeneid* abandoned after one canto
a voyage only known in verse translation
that Ur-journey missed in Garrison Hall
with its wooden desks such tested ships
by passages ventured on Mare Nostrum

o Estevan would not have been pleased
but then he was never to stand in that line

march back & forth at the Varsity Theater
in the movement had its beginning in 1960
for integration of every off-campus movie
seemed harmless enough at the local "Y"
taking part in a meeting held by the SDS
nailing picket signs at the Methodist Center
then holding them up to be taunted & jeered

hurt most by voices from the back of a bus
yelled they didn't need no white boys' help
as if to get even with him in his Mexican jail
had gone to fulfill Moses' colonial dream
those just out to spite whomever they saw
unaware & unconcerned he had gotten off
on figuring it out later so hard to swallow
could not have then since had not yet seen
the book where Barker had set it all down

knew only those rooms he had lectured in
in Garrison on declining Hitt's declensions
or sat in the Old Library named for Eugene
beneath its high beams with stars & angles
reading for the classes that spring semester
the serial novels in pairs assigned by Cline
Russian & Victorian courses taken together
falling asleep in plush brown leather chairs
as lamps cast a soft light on words & floors

reached by marble stairs splotched with gray
a stone found below for those urinals too
the men's with brown-stained wooden doors
one knifed with a dated plea "Susan I need you"
& how did he ever expect her to find it there
even to have heard his biographer lecture

would that have aided in making it through
to have had that history professor explain
how such crises have come & will again

or have listened in Houston & heard him say
to his audience how "Recurrent doubts
are a wholesome antidote to complacency"
would that have made a difference then
when everything led to a pointless end
unlikely unless it might have dawned
how Estevan's very own "Chief" Eugene
had a mind from Riverside & Palestine
though even Christian restored no faith

dropped Mister Enthusiasm's epic class
true epithet for an Aeneas who ever came
armed with anecdotes for all the fates
who had hiked & blocked at Temple High
had as Entellus put on Herculean gloves
but a sense of humor his knockout punch
& after a tennis match or leveling a house
would lift his flute with enormous hands
to balance it at his lips & render an etude

yet would not sit still for listening to Liszt
music of the unwashed with all their kitsch
like Ez rejected loans of an usurious system
ever longed to erect a rammed-earth home
undaunted by strikeout in the game of love
a friend still in deed to his three ex-spouses
did light or heavy repairs around their houses
on visits the kids sleeping crammed among
his Greek & Latin texts his Loeb classics

had Estevan gone back east had any cared
for certain not those who criticized most
their constant resentment reason enough
to have left the reins in ungrateful laps
returned & left them to fend for themselves

always there are others to take one's place
what any man does can be done by another
where then is the honor in suffering through
why bother if fault is found with even the best
& in time a dozen at least may do it better

though none can deny the performance given
in success or failure the learning still earned
never to be taken away nor ever replaced
better be blamed than remain unchanged
from fear too little or too much be said

one student argued against being included
in *Bernie Feldman's Detective Cookbook*
said it would only be thrown in the trash
who never turned in a single assignment
to do or not to do the eternal clash

& if not fated it still seems wholly needful
to descend in indecision to some nether world
to stumble there through each bubbling fosse
for the knowing all those have gone before
their works awaiting whoever would follow

when Webb too met with hopeless moments
would hold up the image of William E. Hinds
& think on books his benefactor sent him
"However much I was tempted to quit

I could not quit without letting him down"

even before the first issue of *Riata* was out
its announced East-West theme under attack
a satirical letter published in the deadly *Texan*
a new cause for thinking would give it all up
when resigning had meant never meeting Jim

no trips to Printing Division on this river street
to approve the plate & later punch the holes
showed in the center of his blind embossing
the rice-paper sheet's burnt-orange smear
reviewed by Ambrose as a collector's item

not to discover Zanders' "Fugue for an Island"
John's story rejected by *New Campus Writing*
then accepted as edited with the title changed
Jim being hired by Printing as a book designer
if not for himself went on for Mary & Moses

but what to do with a disparaging Frantz
has seen Barker's *Life* as far too partial
or with Santa Anna's remark in Castañeda
that Estevan employed an English guile
to trick a generous Mexican nation

can contradict nothing answering the charge
had gathered the material as a despot would
& made that student magazine too prettified
choose rather to re-remember Ransom's call
to come see him at his Chancellor's Office

on his pile carpet before his mahogany desk
stood in awe as he said of that autumn issue

reminded him of *Texas Quarterly* model of all
on the editorial staff he would offer a position
though the necessary funds never came through

while he spent instead the obscene figures
acquiring the works of the dead & buried
authors from Britain France anywhere but here
ignored on Rio Grande St. a Hickey at work
on stories never to grace its expensive pages

ten years later left it for Hudspeth to run
even earlier had started its downhill slide
from halcyon days held Zukofsky & Dickey
with Kim Taylor illustrating their latest lines
then fallen to a versifying of the safest type

in the Tower saw Frances with her aerial view
chain smoking there in her masculine shoes
approached her naively to edit for free
return its past glory helping solicit the new
had no patience she said with the contemporary

blamed her alone for no poem getting in
María declaring it an obsession with print
lusting after another more bolder by-line
in Dante's age if not cardinal a venial sin
she they say kept the academy out of the red

& after all the badmouthing thought & said
let in by Don Miguel would request a review
that omnibus coming out as "Who's Afraid
of the Big Bad Poem?" to feel an absolute fool
yet not at Ransom's behest so never the same

though later on when Bass would up & resign
leave Harry's "center of our cultural compass"
Ransom fulfilled his word in a roundabout way
through revelations gained in on-the-job training
from letters & photos his hoarding had saved

next to Woolworth's at Dacy's Congress St. store
never minded running fill-ins to that dusty stock
yet rather than shelving those slings & pumps
could take down from PRs a blue-covered *Ulysses*
Emerson's trenchant thoughts on Alighieri in PQs

find inspiring quotes in Harry's frontier essays
with immigrant marks notched not on firearms
but in journal jottings of doctors & bookworms
Swante Palm Ashbel Smith Sherman Goodwin:
self-examination "duty insurance" counters sin

forever indebted & if again repaid too late
yet enter in accounts his bringing together
of the manuscript drafts & priceless proofs
as Estevan acted on each stranger's behalf
risked wreckage as well for those to come

two magnets attracted plowman & scholar
& despite the fact of living a century apart
linked in the mind as this river's two forks
by the profit ever from the prophetic force
of their cargoes' hopeful forward thoughts

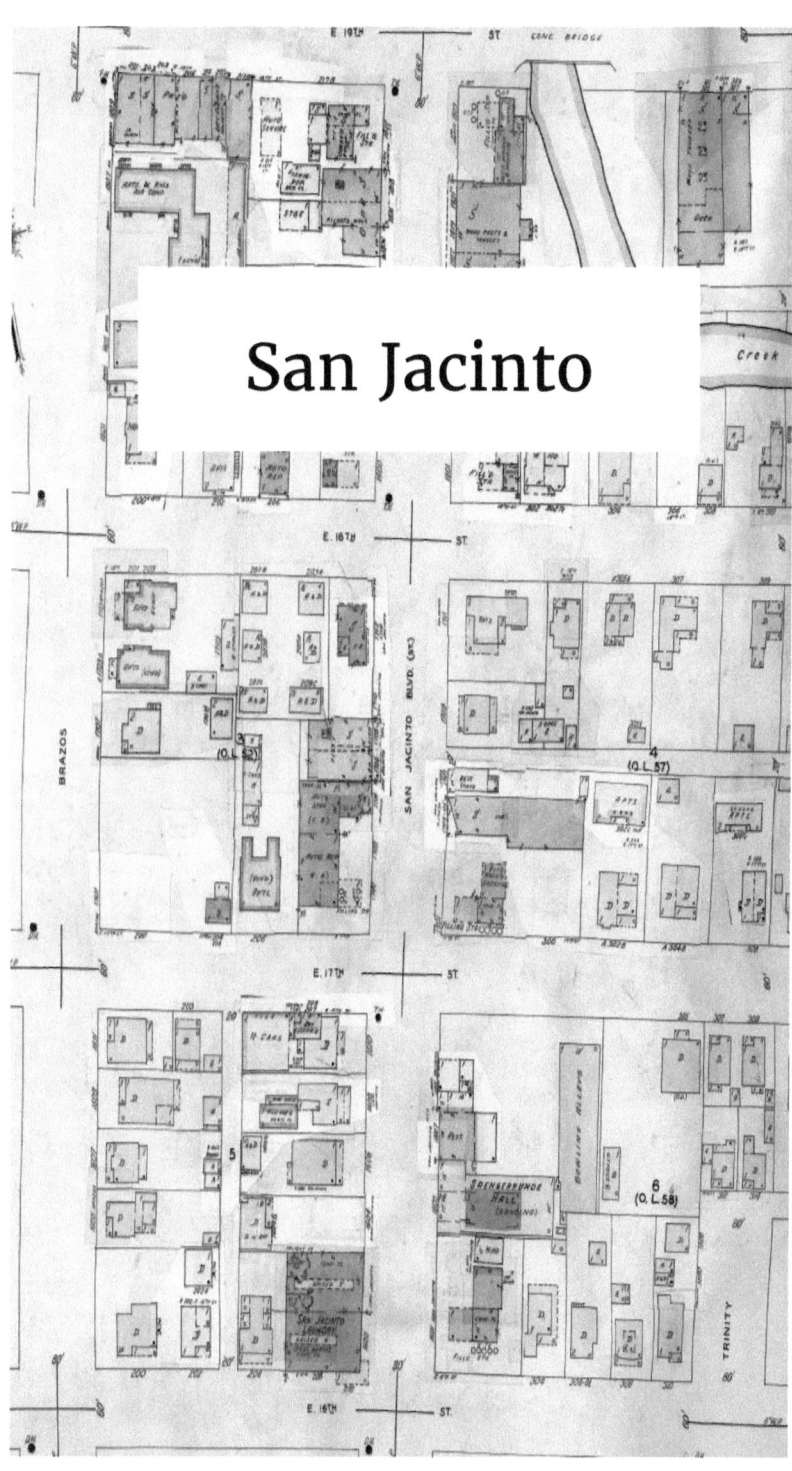

San Jacinto

San Jacinto

      down steps on Memorial Museum's western side
      Proctor's sculpted rearing mustangs symbolize
      "seas of pristine grass   men riding free"
      those borne on their bare or saddled backs
      riding without the ruinous cost of oil & gas

      explorers braves & cowhands plunging ahead
      on Estevan's '29 map whole herds filling up
      the vacant tracks before the searing brands
      of excessive horse sense broke their spirits
      now gone with trails to Alberta & Cheyenne

      while a block south in Memorial Stadium
      Longhorns still dig in for a goal-line stand
      showing what it takes to come from behind
      proving on another crisp autumn afternoon
      how on being down they can turn it around

      always this street conjuring that historic place
      where at siesta time between the silken sheets
      Yellow Rose would give herself for a 36th state
      Sam surprising tented "Napoleon of the West"
      then opposing Austin as governor & capital seat

      yet none of that had mattered to Joseph Jones
      the vituperative troll on his noonday rounds
      who picked from his Waller unsightly plastic
      attacking through inventories in poetic prose
      those from bridge or sidewalks had cast it

      for this city's drainage said more to him
      than any points scored at a championship
      & the only battle he found worthy to fit
      not one pitched at a bayou-headed river

but the struggle to save his campus crick

riffles beside shuttle bus & faculty traffic
as it meanders along with this river street
from museum & stadium to Santa Rita rig
then one fork goes toward Centennial Park
by the Drum & in sight of Hamilton Home

the other continuing toward Scholz's Garten
past pink office buildings of polished granite
the State Library with its anonymous portrait
of Estevan in oil on a window-shade's canvas
to Service on 5th typeset *Life on Waller Creek*

Joe's chapters written on near half-a-century
of sack-lunching to delicate or raucous calls
from the purling water's to wading grackle's
as he observed the ghostly crawfish scuttle
& gathered in the high-carat sunfish gold

counting his riches in the moss's green
as it clung to a slab of fossilized stone
found too from cypress trees' fallen finery
patterns dropped unseen by pecan & oak
sewing their patchwork of light & shadow

first came here in that '60 spring semester
to read in the middle of Joseph's stream
Vanity Fair & alternately *War & Peace*
stretched at length on smooth limestone
with its soothing eddies about & beneath

with their uninvented war one & the same
confused as to characters in which ballroom

unaware of "an old codger" waged his own
against the University's landscape machine
would narrow its lovely water-carved bed

pour concrete on banks & bulldoze its figs
if those to come back as Bobby Layne did
other of its sylvan ancestors unseen again
luscious leaves lost from limbs of trunks
the subject of the troll's outraged lament

his infernal fight making such total sense
his defense of even the lowliest weeds
lobbied to make his creek a garden park
with two gauging stations a record complete
a unique model for the nation to monitor

feared for his city named at first Waterloo
its rill to suffer defeat from dumped refuse
or at hands of careless mindless planners
neo-Bonapartes mapping outlandish growth
a building blitz to overrun its weak position

yet how ban the trashers from Estevan's Eden
generations brought up among cactus & sand
or Elisa from joining in a Tchaikovsky dance
not 1812 cannon but *Nutcracker*'s yule ballet
at the PAC within earshot of Jessen Cascade

where among the string section Darío played
the Brandenburg 6th & Musorgski's *Mountain*
María searched authority files at Public Affairs
& at the HRC raised out of turbulence & haste
able at last to make use of that terminal degree

across from Proctor's statued mustang band
wisterias still twine around their metal posts
their pungent clusters drape as bluish grapes
blooming through each enrollment stampede
& would ever bend toward having them both

on GRE a low score had meant neither one
had it not been for insisting for half an hour
to be given a chance by Hughes acting Dean
to prove through probation could do the work
was not he said material for graduate school

in Battle Hall sat on its forbidding first floor
above his office the library named for Barker
wasn't about to accept any raven's Nevermore
had denied access to Lester's archival bequest
to editing of *Riata* & being chosen for Chile

to find María there at her Binational Center
with an unsecured loan would make it happen
taken out through John Lomax's Texas Exes
then returned to fragrant Batts Hall unforgotten
to form a part of "pool" of assistant professors

each semester before or after classes began
those low-paid temporary contracts renewed
a fortune from having been in '64 barely let in
& able in '76 to make that class assignment
they compose poems seated beside its stream

walked from Parlin Hall across East Mall
to the bridge back of Etter's Alumni Center
where John Lang Sinclair's pep song hangs
on brown butcher paper in his fading hand

passing with the class the site of old B Hall

gone before summer '61 when had sat on grass
watching movies shown at Waggener & in '62
not to cram for that exam in Arab Nationalism
past labs of Schoch founder of Longhorn band
by ROT-C flag then descending fountain stairs

through windblown spray from the jetted water
spilled transparent in view of B. Iden's Theater
named for Payne told Ray who took his course
when he roomed with Andy how Olivier's eyes
look all but dead   see it mostly in his *Hamlet*

Andy at the time into classical *Symphony in C*
Igor's *Rake's Progress* set to an Auden libretto
Fantasticks longest running off-Broadway show
in it Tom Jones parodies that Professor lovingly
an ex-student learned from him as did Rip Torn

in '67 saw him in *Beach Red* with Cornel Wilde
another bloody war film on another Pacific isle
till the Japs a father & son turned suddenly real
snipers in the infested jungles fighting with fear
as invading righteous Marines close in for a kill

saw in the same movie house industrial waste
emptied on the screen & staining a river pink
Perkins in *Pretty Poison* disturbed at his best
a Hobbs picture show only a handful attended
where in a *Volpone* scene María's labor began

brings back again that walk down fountain steps
to the turnaround bridge spans Waller's banks

Austin: a Poem

with that writing class there to watch & listen
among students Arnie Cheryl Peggy Jules Gene
like them would compose from whatever came

a piece on Wukasch mover of Symphony Square
on its stage beside Joe's creek Darío would play
as it rippled between his trio & those would hear
while up the street & stream on another occasion
lunched with Joe & Lord Byron his gimpy friend

watched him hobble but with beak held high
claiming territorial rights in spite of his limp
his feeder with khaki cap & a bag with straps
for collecting the discarded new & old artifacts
his glasses agleam with Waller's reflected light

through willows & vines had climbed with him
clambering over the cypress trees' knobby knees
as he inveighed against racket of cars & mowers
needless motors   men mad for bronzed Bevos
he who had read Neruda seated on Incan stones

who in '44 had begun *The Library Chronicle*
later taken over by Maurer a veritable savior
made it possible to follow them both at HRC
as trimmer of that quarterly's display window
its treasures shown through Caledonia & color

its scraps deposited in this B-Western desert
by Brits & Frogs would soon grow incensed
after laughing their ways to savings & loans
forgetting the Elgin marble & Rosetta stone
with legacies GTT to find the joke on them

can still resent taxes Ransom siphoned there
or so it seemed then & even now will appear
on his leaving so little for the alive & active
who created in this city their books & prints
but would not detract from satisfaction taken

in working with scholars who sent from afar
their posted articles or with a local like Slate
who wrote on that '32 screenplay of *Ulysses*
by Zuk & Reisman with Louis 5 years into *A*
like nightfall Joseph wove it with not a quote

in '77 a class included Ted a student cellist
heard & wrote on the concert of Mahler 5th
had Clare Colquitt then as teaching assistant
her piece printed in '84 on *Contempo* years
an '85 on Edith Wharton letters to *cher ami*

at Duke had met & married Bradford Mudge
who in '83 had contributed his special piece
on Sara Coleridge & her Spanish & Greek
on her editing of her father's difficult texts
on her bout with the family's poppy disease

Irene Rostagno on Knopf & its Latin boom
Carpentier's *Steps* Donoso's *Obscene Bird*
novels & stories from Amazonian backlands
all tracked by her through the files & reviews
ins & outs of the careers of Alfred & Blanche

Rick Lawn on Ross Russell's KC Jazz Style
on his Dial contracts with Schönberg & Bird
& had coaxed Gene Ramey out of retirement
born in '13 beside Waller at 14th & Red River

bassist in on bebop birth with Parker & Monk

Christensen unearthing Olson's song of Worms
in a dark passage of Dahlberg's correspondence
found it slogging his "squalid marshes of wrath"
in "dungy sheepcotes" bitten by his Sodom fleas
then a "dreary impasse" as bottom-dog friends

differing as if a chorus of Edward & Charles
he an Aggie with lines emanated from Bryan
a promoter of Texas poems on his radio show
featuring readers from McDonald to Burford
a Beat Snyder too & Black Mountain Creeley

branded a provincial elitist & charged with bias
on leaving Paul out of that '81 bilingual edition
Cow's Skull a collection of mostly native poets
had excluded him when included other émigrés
who had done for the State poetry so much less

Estevan preferred families over unmarried men
long-suffering not drifters at roundup & harvest
discouraged riff-raff not the industrious debtors
where else go for working off a farm had failed
no first-come first-served basis nor room for all

King denied tenure with three books to his credit
his articles better than enemies would ever admit
on Ezra's library   his triangle with Hilda & Bill
Michael's rich digs for others in Ransom's "theft"
gave release too from tedium of making a living

& with Tom Zigal to have the privilege conferred
of catching & marking typos in galleys & proofs

checking blue lines   correcting footnote or head
contributing regional surveys to his *Pawn Review*
meeting with Luis to discuss *La calavera* & Perú

to have been deprived of Sunder's vital course
on Cabeza de Vaca Catlin Bancroft's Villagrá
Webb's bobwire sixshooter & windmill plains
black dogfaces & cowboys opening the range
the Indians in W.W. Newcomb driven extinct

yet survive in his text on diet of larva & feces
corn & communal hunting running down deer
from ice age to the white man's colder coming
writings on Friedrich Petri & Forrest Kirkland
the two warm exceptions with brushes & pens

like a watercolor & pencil Randall repaired
with the aid of Conservation's fabulous lab
so vicarious & vivid in a way only Petri had
with black boy on horseback turning to look
at a keg of water pulled as a white boy rides

holding by its handle a bucket made of wood
as he passes into cacti out of moss-hung trees
in the background a bonneted mounted figure
races off at breakneck speed as a female black
with basket on her head is bringing up the rear

the Mescalero pictographs Forrest had drafted
from a rock art painted in a Hueco Tanks cave
symbols he drew to save from graffiti & flood
Newcomb would revive & put them into print
from his pages to Inshallah home of Jim Smith

at 43rd & Waller his tradition as host of the arts
where arrowheads still mark their sacred camps
Elisa invited there to shine at her first cast party
from Comanche flints to a daughter in leotards
& the earlier roles played by Bugbee & Barker

said he didn't know why he would even bother
but go on over then to English & see Dr. Crow
said would do no good   he could only agree
so next-door to Parlin to that graduate advisor
where informed at the Office Crow wasn't in

then sent to Dr. Maurer his assistant instead
on knocking greeted by his billy-goat voice
a gruff Come in called through opaque glass
there at his desk Oscar barely lifted his head
just peered in a drawer would open & close

on hearing of Hughes & of Dr. Crow not in
looked hard in the drawer & closed it again
would spot in the pause on one of his walls
the copy of a print by Jon Bracker's friend
Frank Stack etching of a garage apartment

spoke of that & of first meeting Jon in 1960
edited *The Ranger* in its heyday   How is he
in some way from there would bring up jazz
his favorites by far James P. Johnson & Fats
the latter not that Waller paraphrased by Ez

after digressions intriguing as his Trollope's
as he starred at his hands pushing & pulling
he came at last to ask but without looking up
what was needed & hearing a permit to enter

jotted it down & gave it with face still awry

caught on that other surprise & displeasure
as he read the note with Dr. Maurer's okay
a victory impossible with cut-offs & quotas
rents beyond any lower middle-class means
& more so with grades just mediocre at best

to have missed it all by that computed score
but must confess he never slammed the door
though then & there thought it hardly a crack
yet over long haul would open floodgates
as it delivered the store of rivers & streets

the verses & visions in the houses & halls
meditations on Waller as Joseph patrolled
found him alone there still clearing debris
the fallen trees & sewage all backing it up
into foul gray stands of the polluted scum

even as the Committee of full professors
would dam the way for the grant or raise
one in nifty tennis togs & shoes to match
ever ready for sets during his office hour
Joe only at Waller lunchtime or weekend

cleaning the creek that it move & glisten
preserved its creatures for future viewers
for reading of literatures from far & near
taught World English till mandatory age
his lectures teaching a language of flow

let another codger come if only just one
for it takes but a single life vs. the litter

another pupil like him of finest teachers
those like Heraclitus Walton & Thoreau
proffer to the present the lessons live on

for Joe a steward of the wisdom in water
who drew too from its deeps & shallows
a slaking drink of local & distant cultures
ever taking its history as a rod to measure
the insatiable thirst for fuel & horsepower

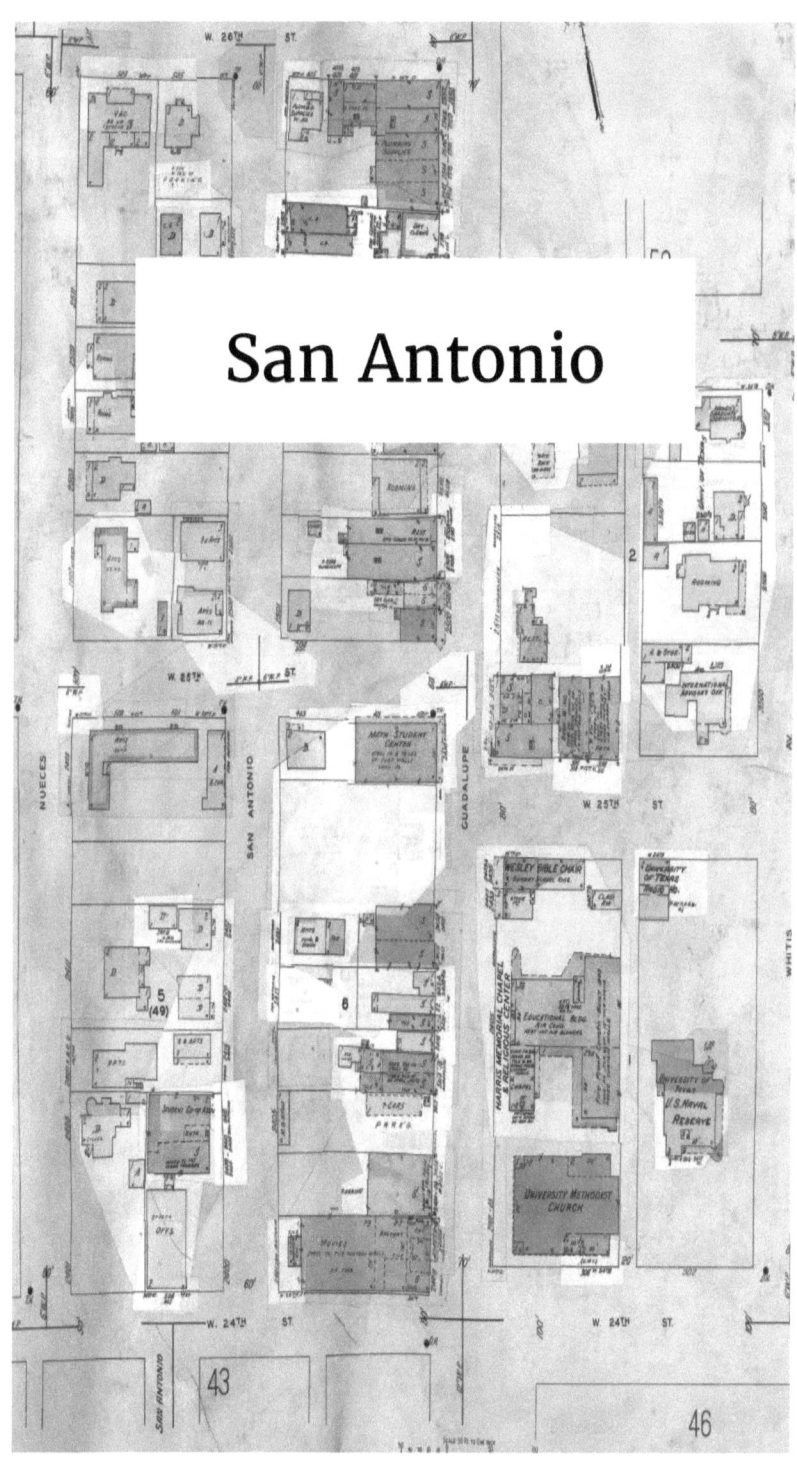

San Antonio

Austin: a Poem

San Antonio

at 21st & this river street
with the playground empty
& its wire gates opened wide
have crossed the asphalt often
where during their hour outside
her classes dodged or shot the ball

at not much more than four-foot tall
at Saint Austin's where once she taught
in the Paulist Fathers' parochial school
was towered over
by the 5th- & 6th-grade boys
yet in the little she wrote never came up short

at Goliad
the superior marksmen
were surrounded & caught
in an open field
then surrendered their arms
with cover & food in nearby woods

at twenty-seven in '74
mysteriously dead in Ecuador
had disappeared in Guayaquil
then weeks later washed ashore
onto the beach she had walked alone
repeating new poems shall never hear

at the mercy of artillery pieces
their carbines surrendered for dreams
of arriving back across the Sabine
both wounded & whole of return
all of a joyous reunion
with their wives & children

at sight of their playground
think again of her
& of her lines this city has lost
like bars of gold
in a galleon sunken off the coast
no salvage crew will ever float

at her going knew
more than most
of the naked heart & soul
& of "what remains
when one is stripped
of all accoutrements"

at even her height & age
had seen above most
for through her poet's tongue
her body's highest organ
had spoken upon
"Is not Was nor Will Be"

at thirty Fannin still brash
from their resounding defeat
of Mexican troops his own sent reeling
though by them outnumbered 60 to 1
ordered to attack & then to retreat
in vacillation branded a coward & traitor

at the moment of love
she describes a descent
to the kingdoms of
animal mineral & plant
"all we once were"
& "whence we come"

at his erectile pointing
felt & pictured in four directions
the two as "one wonderful well-oiled machine"
herself the "Borealis all afire"
not knowing where his compass ended
& her magnetic north began

at Urrea's hands
clemency had seemed assured
yet Santa Anna unconvinced
instructed instead most be marched
along the upper & lower fords
& lined up there for slaughter

at a loss to say
how high a pint-sized Susan Lucas
no salt-dome gusher
might have reached
in living longer
could hardly hazard a guess

at this corner of kicks
& yells of recess
can only recall her distant walk
low & unaccommodated as nuncle Lear
yet even with less of her bullion left
out grades any player twice as tall

at the commotion & smoke
28 would escape among the mesquite
drift down the river names this street
to a fate she came to share
by the intersection of her poetry
with those remembered 300 & more

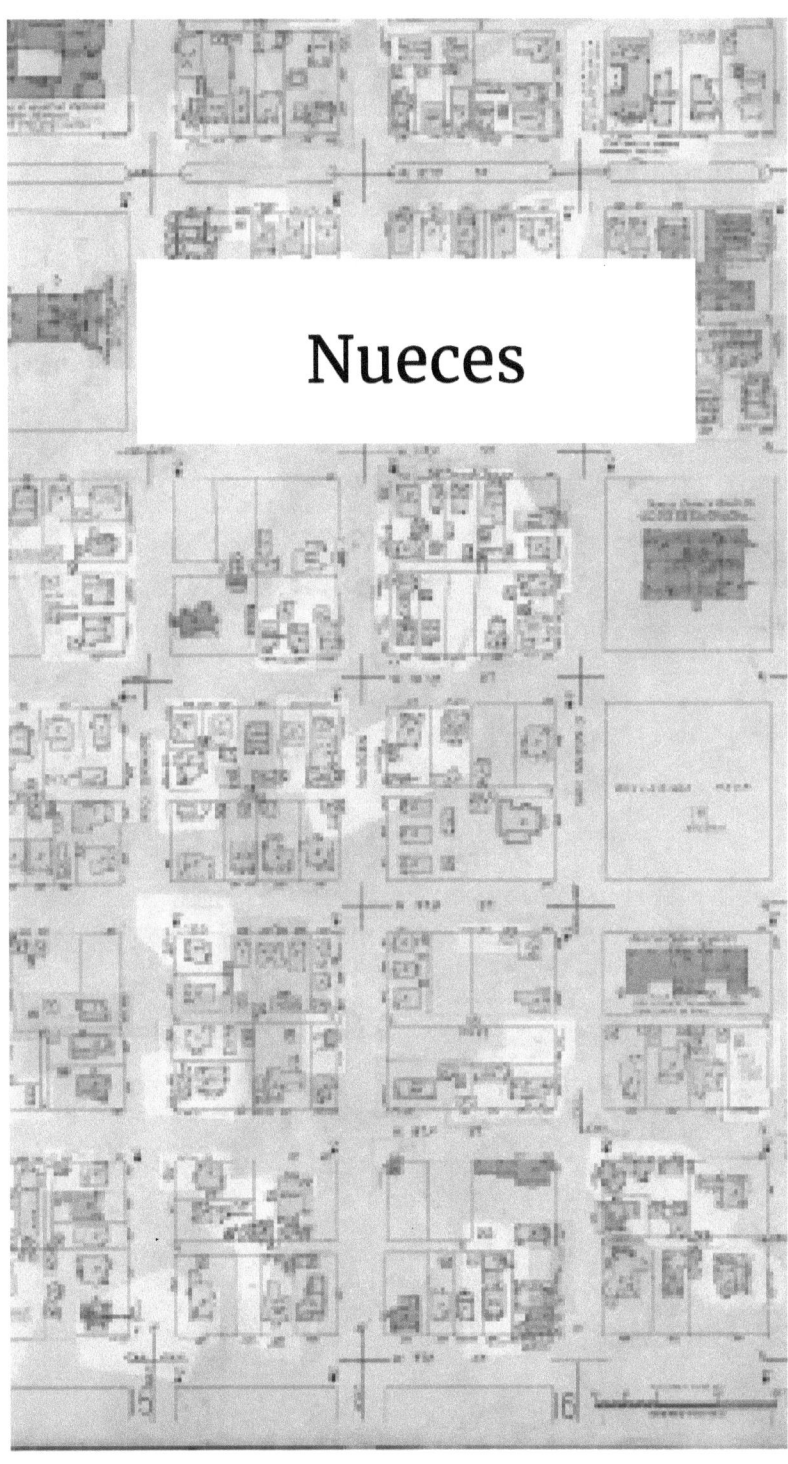

Nueces

Nueces

was this the street where Donnie stayed
favorite of Granny Polk on Daddy's side
who dropped off his date near Forest Park
slid on a wet curve lost control & died
Tommy after delivering his Green Berets
flipped & crushed under the steering wheel
that cousin first & then that only brother

on coming in '56 those losses still remote
later in decade to find this city a sanctuary
one flown to year-round by migrating minds
with its environment conducive to idea & art
but found Donnie's fraternity in mourning then
for a member dead in a wreck the night before
his wake held on Lavaca at the Scottish Rite

its windowless walls mysterious as death
walked past them from downtown to campus
after arriving that first trip by Greyhound bus
a representative then for Boy Scouts Week
put up at Bergstrom in the Air Base barracks
attended a Union ball where Sinclair's "Eyes"
still peer across West Mall to Architecture

stood looking on as the cute couples danced
thrilled to be a part though ever at a distance
if future times & friends not dimly perceived
felt nonetheless somehow this city's heartbeat
the wonder of those Commons looming ahead
gathering there for hearing with Hickey's circle
his pronouncements so outrageous & o so subtle

there in '62 Franklin Haar going over his poems
typed with inkless ribbons on coffee-stained sheets

in '77 caught with a class phrases for *The Poet Trap*
"heavy with Hamburger fog" "rehearsals downbeats"
those of Laura & Renee listened to a brass quintet
played where Shirley Bird Perry had Jesson engrave
limestone emblems above its remodeled entrance

to longhorn mocker jack rabbit & cactus
horned frog & owl a prairie dog a rattler
added rook & knight masks comic & tragic
harp & lute along with quill brush & palette
festive grapes opened text & a swaying nude
all embraced among learning's leaves & fruit
but then it may not have even been Nueces

& yet that first day still distinctly comes in
to Webb his clear as "pictures on a screen"
but set to record three unforgettable precepts
left on his typewritten page an unfilled space
have located two vacant lots two blocks apart
one for certain right where Walter first lived
when from MK&T he took a streetcar north

on the other a frat house the city condemned
razed in later years after its members hazed
even kicked & pissed on a passing student
would that have been that cousin's then
Webb as a frosh in on a sophomore's shooting
a fight in '12 brought passage of a hazing law
but failed to save a Corps cadet died in '84

each on a corner   the Greeks' at 24th
Walter's at 22nd   two such distant worlds
the former's brick now reduced to rubble
but thanks to all John Morris's trouble

the latter transported to a garbage heap
where goats then grazed on native grass
with windows in view of Balcones Fault

& whose if not of one & all
have failed to read or ever to right
past or present for the future's sake
will leave it for a John to sacrifice
for knowing where Webb first wrote
recalls too across & down this street
Bugbee came to rescue Estevan's repute

its panels a history of tongue & groove
of "pumpkin" pine made tung-oil smooth
porcelain knobs on doors of a perfect fit
in '80 before Webb would room & board
kids by height scribbling their arithmetic
on Miss M.V. Jones's Select School walls
early solutions for any would double-check

those John recovered by his detective love
as too Pompee's fine hand-slotted frame
wheelwright's 1875 German-French design
remodeled & added to circa 1880 or '79
to preserve it John to lose wife & daughter
Anne preferring IBM & the corporate gains
from her had first learned a bit of Russian

would lead to shores of Pushkin's poem
with its bronze horseman's stately Neva
grown restless with wind & a backing sea
he as a bedridden invalid tosses & turns
till it rises & drives its wedge of water
between Yevgeny & his dearly beloved

John's restoration become a Nueces in flood

such pain of separation relieved by spraying
the Wright's pavonia an endangered species
by watching garden stones darken with wet
bacon & alibates flint for lightening the day
dogtooth jasper chalcedony calcite crystals
copper cedar roots strips of petrified wood
varieties of cactus all experts on survival

his own spirits lifted on dampening those
on observing the colonies of lichen thrive
the patient decades it took them to build
their green encampments on barren fields
plowed under by developers in an afternoon
forced again to move his matrimonial house
by those would profit from his secluded home

odyssey of the place where Webb composed
country boy wrought up by magic meaning
of words set down in their orderly rhythm
with a music for those then & those to come
though a writing course did not recommend
just wide reading bridge building hoboing poker
well-drilling lovemaking windjamming war

John a model in that historian's mold
reared on the range up near Amarillo
from here to Houston drove moving vans
like Terry Raines the native printer
had done it himself whatever it was
John's Russian major "oh it's nothing much"
Terry's geodesic dome "anyone could've"

such unassuming manners o so sicken
how ever hope even to master English
any mechanical failure can hardly fix
those salvage repair resurrect & restore
Terry reusing scrap for his outside stairs
joists from a demolished university roof
iron from Seton   he Brackenridge born

who grants to things their second chance
will allow an elevator door to rise again
the rejected pillars to support once more
who explores a Texan or a Mexican cave
the cool of his own deep modest ways
while John underneath a newer veneer
discovers a house's date & truer color

Terry in his stand of cedar & oak
on one side of a grassy arroyo bed
just off the Kyle to Wimberley road
constructed a bunk & woodstove cabin
facing a tree-topped limestone ledge
its bathroom put in without a door
left open to creek & passing deer

from lumber & a telephone pole
he built it first with its lighted path
leads to where the print shop's now
to a pond dammed up & rocked about
stocked with ducks & sodded around
from a sturdy trunk ran a cable down
to slide from slope to refreshing splash

had only begun just beyond the rise
a two-storey house of his own design

its shell to become his & Suzy's home
living meanwhile atop his circular shop
in a windowed room above the grove
as its changing leaf tones come & go
he at sundown reading or at the piano

in work boots & his plaid flannel shirt
with his cap on & his sun-tanned face
with nicked glued & ink-stained hands
plays Bach inventions on a baby grand
between his Heidelberg two-color runs
& burning of plates for an overdue job
collating & binding & trimming it out

so exasperating with his constant delays
at midnight Jim redoing a dummy again
re-moving the head & re-spacing a line
waited on both with a shortened fuse
shooting off before recoil of remorse
knowing this pair got the poetry read
a layout & printing to match the muse

the two in doing so paying the price
or kids & ex-wives bearing the cost
a son ever uncertain to whom to turn
for years not touching nutritious food
would eat no veggies no salad nor fruit
dropped out of schools public or private
tried this tried that friendless & confused

with fresh spring or cool fall mornings
daughters born before the oval bedroom
waking to another stranger sleeping over
to mothers cooking meals in a rusting bus

still parked within sight of a latest live-in
summers split between parental dreams
immolation on altars of idyllic communes

though Bugbee & Estevan knew none of this
for Lester no marital but misery of Fort Bliss
having tied no knot just stuck to his books
balanced the accounts & wrote them down
for those thereafter would inherit the land
or those later on would wish to discover
who tilled it first   who ran with the ball

saved newspaper clippings & cut out ads
collected a flyer with Rootatorial cheers
recorded the Longhorns' clever dodging
when Varsity boys laid it on Houston's ten
knocked their whole line into smithereens
with Bethea scoring behind that Texas wall
though "Wortham failed on every easy goal"

when gowns cooperated with citizens of town
& a fullback sang in the University Quartette
the program included a mandolin & violin trio
Bugbee even retaining their sheet music parts
from Hancock Opera House a *Ben-Hur* handout
two photos of Walt Whitman at ages 53 & 68
one of Gladstone gave Lester his middle name

even preserved Dr. Dayton's doggerel song
"The first of the villains who came to this state
Was runaway Stephen F. Austin the great!"
made deeply sad by friends' good intentions
men tarred & feathered in the leader's absence
of the Colony's first two years Bugbee notes

just one case of theft not a single homicide

& would register the amount Estevan asked
for his services to colonists in want of cash
willing to take any property not "a dead loss"
horses mules cattle furs peltry beeswax hogs
dressed deer skins or homemade cloth
"will sacrifice my own interest rather
than distress them for one red cent"

out of his own pocket a draftsman paid
to plot the tract each deed called for
"The great expenses voluntarily incurred
must forever free him from the charge
sounds like sarcasm to speak of defrauding
'shook off the Yoke and dispersed the cloud
had so long kept his settlers in the dark"

"Bugbee from even slenderer means
advanced money for labor and postage
to solicit *Quarterly* members by mail"
"grew to manhood in Johnson County
the post oak & black jacks of Cross Timbers
on the southwest fringed by the Brazos River"
"1890-91 lived at 2110 August St. now Nueces"

only "avoidable expense" his occasional trip
to visit the theatre for catching a Salvini
an Irving Terry in *Merchant of Venice*
his family concerned he had joined a fraternity
his mother sending extra money now & again
never telling the father who was so far in debt
"made 18 bales but won't come out much ahead"

like Webb went off later for the advanced degree
Walter never wanted to leave & said he believed
to have stayed in state had been far better off
a silly superstition to him such going away
said Oxford & Cambridge great from being inbred
on the train home after he had flunked his doctoral
luxuriated in a soft Texas voice's welcome drawl

at Columbia Bugbee worked his way with ease
through the academic details massed to impede
but physicians' bills & the chronic school fees
his dear mother's death & his efforts to lessen
his sister's monotonous days back on the farm
forced his return before he had made it through
here to a pitiful salary with his time running out

always his classes prepared with exhaustive care
would never lecture but move from desk to desk
questioning & discussing each student's response
after the bell all would gather about him for more
taking precious minutes from his unfinished Life
one recalled his winding & rewinding the chain
of a watch had gone ticking relentlessly amain

"In looking back I know now that over
and over again Bugbee's sound judgment
his knowledge of human nature   patient
and persistent insistence
that young men may be led
but not driven
saved from disaster the B Hall experiment"

his allotment of a mere six active years
ended as the century turned to nineteen-one

in Woodbury near Hillsboro his studies had begun
had taken part there in various debates: Resolved
That woman has more influence over man than money
"walked to Pleasant Point for the mail and received
a searching letter from DAISY declaring our friendship over"

That the white man has a better right to the States
than the Indian   That works of art are more attractive
to the eye than nature   at Mansfield College
wrote "Queer Queries":   What is the "River of Blood"?
Answer Colorado: — signifying "bloody water"
from Horace copied none's content with his own occupation
yet no one will exchange positions with another

had entered the University January 1887
family resources stretched for the second semester
"along the line took an introductory course in the language
he was to use most in his subsequent investigations"
Spanish discouraged in 1960s the choice German or French
declared no important literature written in it since Cervantes
yet in February '65 to discover Parra's antipoems in *Motive*

a vein opened up through that Undergraduate periodicals
     room
another lodestone would draw towards what richness to come
under classical quotations at Main symbolled rafters at Barker
to read the lines & stanzas there & to take passage once more
sinking in seats & hearing that antipoetry ring true
moments placed in settings let them happen over & over
secret mine shafts revealed   when & where the clue

pulled later to Alonso Ercilla Blest Gana & Pezoa Véliz
Huidobro Mistral Neruda & Lihn   then on to Cuba
& the three trapped tigers of Cabrera Infante

Carpentier's enlightenment   Lezama Lima's paradiso
Macondo of García Márquez   Mexicans Rulfo Pacheco & Paz
the Tiresias affair in Borges   Sábato Puig & Cortázar
Marios of Montevideo   Vargas Llosa's green house in Perú

in San Felipe Estevan had established first
instruction in English but of prime importance
the teaching of other of the modern tongues
"and especially of Spanish"   from a cholera attack
would not recover   gone by the end of 1836
in March '35 had written under the clouds of war
to tell Perry to "keep the children in school"

debunked by John Henry Faulk on public TV
as first real estate agent offered the others' lands
on lowest terms   as the world turns
Estevan's demeanor takes on a look so sinister & cubist
his cross-eyed view of the darker as a barbaric race
"the enemy prepared to enlist the Negroes free or slave"
a serious threat to the peerless civilized white

statements made as health & patience gave way
but to Faulk just another enterprising racist
his passport to a promised land stamped nil & void
more a Moses forbidden entrance than his father before
reduced to a writer of ads & clever commercials
adept at attracting & luring as in later years
the high tech biz of Silicon Valleys & MCIs

in defense think quickly of athletic John Seals
linebacker offensive guard & philosophy major
on the first team recruited by Darrell Royal
had run wind sprints with a fractured fibula
now pediatric neurologist reads Johnson & Blake

Austin: a Poem   117

in '60 to wear his jersey to Silber's Plan II class
knowing full well that Dean abhorred the sport

Bugbee a booster both of the jocks & poets
close associate of Ed Blount & Hans Hertzberg
two "completely Bohemian in taste & conduct"
Blount later a dermatologist never happy he said
except in some dream-world creating his poems
French imitations or based them on Grecian stones
filled them with nightingales he had never seen once

took imagery from most anywhere but his Hillsboro home
never from this city nor even from the Forty Acres
the closest an Arkansas scene from his passing train
yet Bugbee would send his verses to publishing firms
in between the History I & II exams he gave each term
"After 350 A.D. to what provincial official would an order
to organize an expedition against the Picts be addressed?"

Hertzberg's "Would-Be Epic" *Lawyers and Laurels*
subtitled "Didactic History of the Junior Law Class"
printed here in 1891 by Eugene Von Boeckmann
more the sort of thing Bugbee must have hoped to read
who wrote for young men & women not to by-pass
their own University for some out-of-state college
"From every point of view this is undesirable

prevents the youths from becoming thoroughly imbued
with ideals obtaining" in their own backyards
"becoming thoroughly acquainted with resources
interests and the people of their own community"
must have cherished Hans's use of place names
a town or city for each classmate's special quality
"Young oak from Oakland a pine tall Tyler son of toil

Smith of Fort Worth fond of Tennis & Tennyson
makes much of racket & ball
but's sometimes silent in the Junior Hall"
those who tow the law & toe the waltz equally
"May they cut in life's quadrilles capers gracefully"
the short of stature but stentorian tongued
those first come in low then finish on highest rung

"Thro' meadows brooks in placid clearness flow
Without wild roaring or tempestuous show
So does our Junior Brooks' balanced brain
Work steady on
And 'shyster lawyer' will never soil his name"
of himself the poet will only say "am not thus vain
As to speak self while better men remain

The harp strings break in twain—
Ne'er will they breathe such melody again!
Ne'er was a theme so genial to my heart
Ne'er was it so hard from any theme to part"
then left it all for the Windy City
fell down an elevator shaft "grievously crippled"
his *Century* rejection slip the final crushing blow

Hans' *Lyrics of Love* a "poetaster's ill-tuned lyre"
while Bugbee changed the tone of historical writing
visited Colonel Bryan owned the Austin archive
"stored in a tower room at his home in Quintana
to protect [it] from inundation by Gulf storms
more precious to him than a heritage of gold"
made headway on the Life then had to give it up

Barker convinced it would have been brilliant
but had to travel to Junction for his failing health

his case diagnosed at Fort Bliss as tuberculosis
prescribed "rigorous exercise" as suitable care
"Despite their high appreciation of his services
the regents had no power to continue his [pay]
and the tragic pity was that he needed" it so

"I am living a pretty hard life in El Paso
In Austin I at least deluded myself
into thinking that I passed for *somebody*
bank presidents would bow cordially
freshmen tip their hats   girls beam beamingly
but now as I pass along I hear
there goes another lunger   need a city ordinance

to keep them away   Have been packing grapes
with a family near Isleta   made with Dr. Baird
microscopic examinations   miss the classes
research on the Colony   can't imagine the University
on opening day   to be there when it starts
but to take no part"   at the banks of the Rio Grande
on March 17 1902 died two months shy of 33

his hero of pneumonia at 43
in a December cold in his unheated shack
that last month there would belatedly draft
his proclamation against the slavery trade
but the damage done & then Bugbee gone
had just begun to save his rightful place
many with longer life with less to show

most with regrets for days they wasted
the owed unpaid a love left unexpressed
points of unsettled arguments unrecalled
some with no heirs to follow in their steps

others with offspring would later question
stands not taken or reject those that were
all they long stood for & abided to bring

must await another to gird on the sword
would seek in truth no revenge of time
come rather to recover the candid words
to copy documents & set records straight
both those written & the ways they lived
if self-justified yet needful & deserving of
a Barker born *en buena hora   un mío Cid*

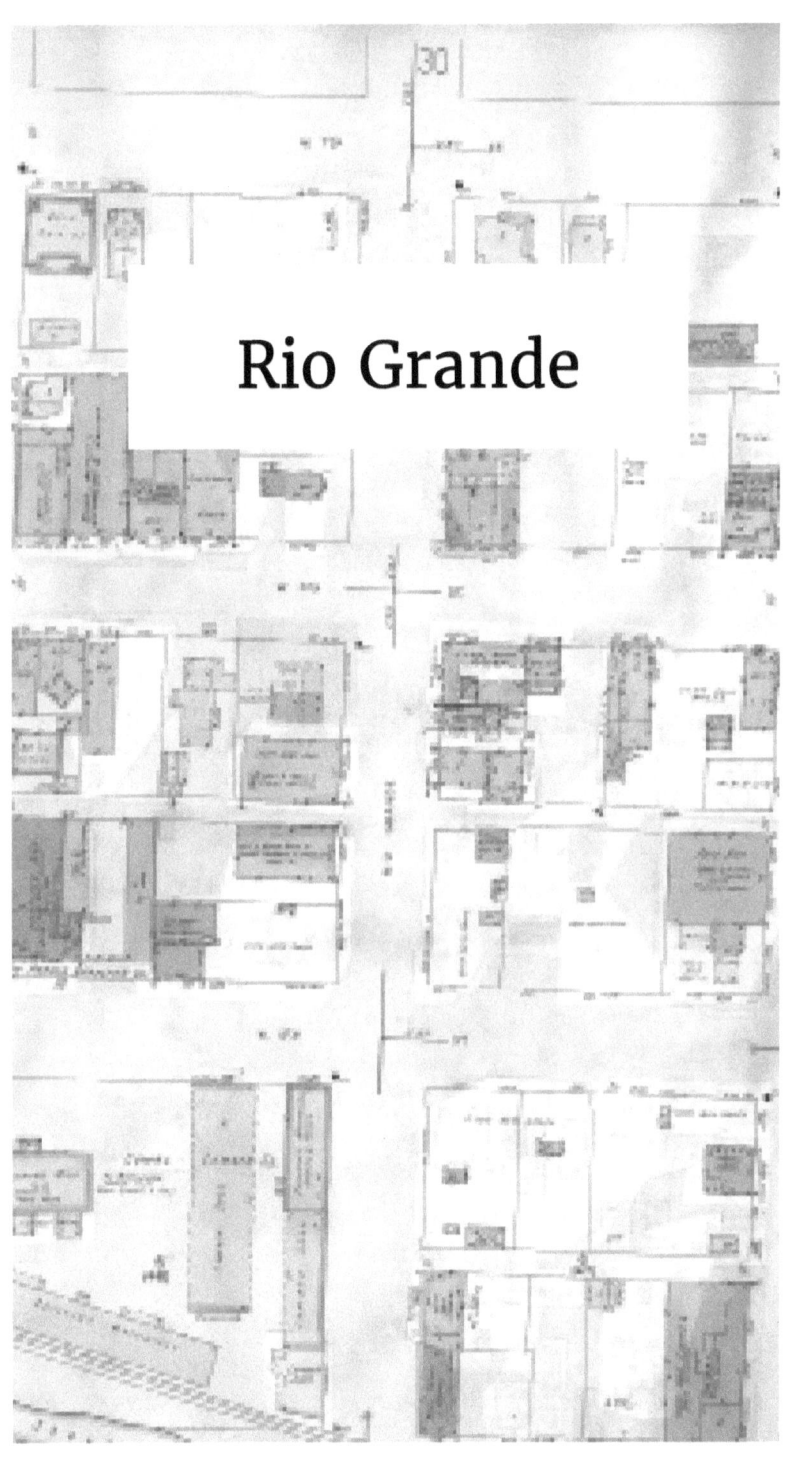

Rio Grande

Austin: a Poem

Rio Grande

came never intending to leech off friends
but stayed for a week & then half a year
cannot remember how or who invited
only where & why each yet stands clear
from sleeping there on a daybed between
a space heater & that back porch screen
with its plastic sheet flapped all night long
from the autumn & then the winter wind
one side freezing & the other done
merely existing at 2300 Rio Grand'
with a realer romantic self still in Chile
from where in September had just returned
there but a month though it seemed as if
had never left   working at Dacy's to earn
for a trip would rejoin those divided selves
so ready once more to quit this city
where at 23rd would watch in years to come
Elisa practice her first *tendu* & *entrechat*
bending & stretching at the wooden bar
lifting & rising toward the balletic art
an inconceivable gift María would give
but then unknown as was Estevan's day
when he & afterwards President Lamar
had created the schools & laid out roads
would pave the way for her training here
her slowly preparing for pains on *pointe*
knew only to toss & turn from hot to cold
on that mattress a thrall to such paradox
gripped by fears of how when or even if
by an icy lust smoldered deep within
for another with whom it wasn't meant
yet wondrously drawn to hurry back
through all that wrong to find at last
the rightness of a ballerina born of her

whose *pas de chats* to piano strains
would bring her close as half a block
at ABT her classes first with Joanie
then after the studio had moved to 5th
with Lisa Smith feather light as Juliet
& later still at Ballet Austin on Guadalupe
studying with Miss León & Mrs. Loomis
in renovated Hose Company Station No. 6
never guessing then nor half surmising
the wars they fought with Santa Anna
Lipan Apache Karankaway & Comanche
the taxes levied & their soles replaced
would lead to a daughter's graceful steps
ignorant then of Estevan's love repressed
his journey ending on a procrustean bed
his sacrifice unrecognized for all it's worth
only crossed this river street back & forth
sweating the German & Government tests
concerned Verónica would never care
had abandoned place & people all for her
felt even then as Lamar though unaware
when Mirabeau invaded Doña Carlota's land
marched to Monterrey from the Rio Grand'
to save that nation from its "erring mind"
by a sense of duty torn & pulled both ways
by her he had lost with his valiant sword
"But wo is me / Between us roars a gloomy stream"
while Villagrá captain-poet with Oñate's men
had paddled against its fateful current
trekked fiery sands no Christian had trod
where the briars & nets of stinging twigs
lashed at eyes & ripped at unarmored legs
their bare swollen feet at the mercy of
the scabrous rocks & high hot dunes

for more than fifty days marched on & on
for seven straight in a drenching rain
at the end of a final four without a drop
in their haste the horses would overdrink
with their flanks filled had died "satisfied"
men blinded by dagger sun & piñon lance
some wading out too far then swept away
by a wealth of waters could not believe
the troops spread out along its banks
like bloated toads or tavern drunks
all this river to them not near enough
to slake their parched & voiceless throats
then shown at El Paso a convenient ford
by barbarians with the crudest of instincts
who hunted & fished & lived off roots
never breaking earth or planting seeds
unconcerned grand cities grew in far León
ignored the stir of palace or highest court
nor had they ever had to face red tape
impediment to Oñate's moving ahead
delayed for months by jealous hatred
uncouth contented unsuspicious brutes
leading them across at the very point
where border guards would stop the car
on coming back from the Júarez shops
with a black sheep cousin & his Chicana wife
María with Darío still breast-feeding then
when the officer stooped to search inside
to ask "Is everyone here a U.S. citizen?"
she a registered alien would answer Chilean
when the trouble & rude treatment all began
with her card left in Hobbs could not come in
she & the baby must remain on that other side
"But wo is me / Between us roars a gloomy stream"

phoned to friends told them just break in
ransack the house but find that Card
the Green with her picture she detested so
whose magic numbers could part Red Seas
would let them pass over & bring them back
the two kept in Mexico by more than water
so cruelly cut off by the indifferent law
while passage to her & her Santiago home
enabled by those roomed on this river street
its Spanish name a link to her long thin land
its blocks strolled with friends or all alone
as on visits to Gilliam's Brickrow shelves
at 1913 on the corner somehow of 21st
that Book Shop with its Howells & Hardy
bought there & read those first 1st editions
a volume of Spenser introduced by Yeats
Wm. Dean's novel *The Shadow of a Dream*
like the one fell on Estevan ever & again
along the way lost all but *Moments of Vision*
never thinking those too were there & then
on that Hardy end sheet wrote "Austin '61"
had gone there with proper & superior Jon
by misted sidewalks with their fallen leaves
would stick to the heels of his size thirteens
shrill grackles whistling in bare-limbed trees
their wet black branches a darkening against
the gray-orange-pink of autumn's sunset sky
gave hope even here poems might come to life
before the nights on Hickeys' screened-in porch
when Mary Jane had tired of seeing a poet-type
asleep out there or in their kitchen scribbling
or ironing a dress shirt for work each morning
she cooking Dave's breakfast & chatting a bit
being civil but thinking Why doesn't he leave

yet stayed on through fall '65 & into winter
a nuisance to them & yet would always pay
but how could 25 dollars ever cover the sight
of a freeloader there when they returned at night
passing through that "bedroom" to enter their own
had at least used toilet & shower offered by Lonn
in his garage apartment back of their big 2-storey
next door to Leslie who would loan her phone
a bother to all & yet they would put up with
the savings made & the moonings for love
in the meantime butt of their Elephant jokes
later on would appropriate the Spiller & Baugh
those expensive hardback literary histories
could feel no rancor on losing such books
since not even those would ever repay
the inconvenience of such a worn-out stay
can only hope in a way this compensates
if those times with all their impositions
their kindnesses & "moments of vision"
bring back at least a painful pleasure
beyond imbursement of a monetary kind
by allowing these sketches of former days
to make small return for all they gave
for theirs as worthy if written up right
as the lives & letters in that reference set
Hickey in cowboy boots & blue-jean pants
all he would wear except for his Stetson
as he would polish again each paragraph
in between lift his bare mole-ridden back
to catch in a heave his second breath
like his hero Fitzgerald unable to spell
signed up for a course to get some help
his name spotted on a remedial roll
by Dean took away his assistantship

afterwards held forth at Student Union
on the latest theories linguistic or fictive
or holed up at their house on Rio Grand'
to sit day or night in its book-lined study
taking deep drags or swigs from Pepsis
closing sliding doors to shut himself in
for writing & typing his Texas stories
of buttering tortillas or hunting quail
the authentic life & death of Smiley Logan
who at 12 hit Odessa's National Bank
at 25 by a truck load of underfed steers
his best of a San Antonio TV newsman
a Jewish ambulance chaser meets his match
in the Mexican mother of George Guzmán
who views his slow dying filmed & shown
unflinching in the face of a car wreck's jaws
her son caught between them & pinned inside
for her the reporter's re-run a liturgical song
as if a priest Garland Marlinberg offering it up
such scenes Hickey meant for the magazines
The Atlantic   Harper's   The New Yorker
looked ever East for the acceptance signs
gave it all up after they had not arrived
his tale of a nude rancher dies in his tub
listed in McMurtry's *In a Narrow Grave*
though merits a place on this roll call more
for bringing them out as Estevan before
lines & pages of native & immigrant alike
edited for *Riata* & given welcome at home
where artists & authors all gathered to meet
came in a steady stream to this river street
prose & pigment talk overflowing the rooms
their canvases hung where Mary Jane served
as gracious host to the unwashed anarchists

Gilbert Shelton showing off his latest t-shirt
featured Wonder Wart Hog's bristling snout
known too for drawing that satirical Ranger
a stunted Hairy with those holstered six-guns
such figures he had created for serial cartoons
their comments made in social & political fun
or with Hairy pictured on that *Ranger* cover
peering up at a Mona Lisa bore his ugly mug
in its caption spouting to the museum guard
he didn't know nothin' 'bout no *modren* art
but by god he knew he liked what he saw
& Jaxson's underground *Rag* the nation's first
was it he who drew that so classic strip
of the finger-lickin' good fried chicken
of Maddox who wields his racist wood
whose attitude toward his Negro cook
gets radically adjusted by Super Good
but not before hero's battered & bruised
by Lester's axe-handle response to protest
when a light bulb appears over Super's head
with a black indelible ink will dye the bigot
& so many others like Beeson & Osborn
Harold writing "A Matter of Possession"
in a room rented together summer of '63
around the block from the Robert E. Lee
from a bar Mort would regularly frequent
after practice walking by Littlefield on 21st
with its web-footed horses & sudsy fountain
stopping for a longneck & a large sour pickle
then home by watered lawns of frail landladies
tough customers those when came time to collect
ran their musty boarding houses on the up & up
served creamed cauliflower & plenty of spuds
but couldn't hold out against the push for space

another house & street forever displaced
another memorial address made to give way
buildings leveled won't matter to most
but will hold to their images all the more
will not let go though there's not a trace
recall Harold's tale in *Riata* winter of '63
of Sugar & Turpin who are both released
just as Clarence's turn has come at last
to claim as his throne their jail cell's chair
though its meaning lost with those not there
when he rips off the legs & kicks in the seat
burns them all in laughing hysterical defeat
& Carolyn's character in "Ancient History"
her early story from the spring issue of '64
crazy old Miss Agnes Doyle tells a prissy girl
hell no she don't have no telephone
& all you need's a good switchin'
declares "of the two kinds of not knowing
not knowing where you've been is worse"
Hickey printing others by Branda & Giles
not then Jim's tale of Whitman's "August Day"
came later with its "landscape of Spanish-brick
fountains and statuary ranging from lifeless"
to "the bloody mangled bodies in his wake"
but rather the poems of Wally Stopher the 3rd
& of Tom Whitbread who sat one night
on the edge of that daybed there out back
with a party at the Hickeys' roaring inside
at the time he had not then given it up
after a few speaking under the effects
of what it was much too sleepy to catch
perhaps of the trains he so truly loved
can still hear his lines from *Triad* issue 3
take to task the *Harper's* "reporter/distorter"

of these streets & of Texas Eagle's diner car
Wally last seen bound east on a campus shuttle
snaggletoothed & needing the price of a string
said without a guitar it kept him from singing
wondered without his teeth had his talent gone
or with less to begin with had been better off
picking up hints instead from all these others
or as laureate Barney had written "for a song"
in these "certain discoverable neighborhoods"
here on Estevan's river & his numbered streets
or from another contributor like Mueller Lewis
whose "Homespun Idyll" still haunts & weaves
how Buddo turns from spider to a victim trapped
by the triumph of his own sabotage's subtle web
or from Eldon who rediscovered Christina Stead
& for *The Handbook of Texas* set his novel aside
then caught up for ten years in reviewing the facts
in verifying names of odd townships owed to him
& Frigyes Karinthy's "Circus" translated by Fono
after escape from his Hungary invaded by tanks
on Rio Grand' one & all received & accepted
& later on 12th St. at Hickey's gallery named
after "Papa'"s "A Clean Well-Lighted Place"
like a selfless Estevan promoting their work
but then up & left it for old New York
where predictably lost her to the tempting Apple
his lovely Eve from Midland-Odessa
with her deep accent forever distinctive
its desert sweetness so clear & clean
not oil slick as her Permian Basin
but welling up as if artesian
rich in its unassuming ingenuous ring
looked back after another big business trip
an exhibit in Chicago Nashville or Omaha

saw her in one of those lonely office halls
& watched as his Eurydice half disappeared
into a known attorney's awaiting arms
saw too his own employment evaporate
as an agent for the age's pop-art rage
that famous Irish quote his parting shot
at the boss who had double-crossed
Hickey & all of his painter friends:
"the ship abandoned a sinking rat"
while Estevan never left except to carry
his colony's case to a Congress in session
giving up his plans for erecting a house
for Mary Holley & for hearing her voice
as he dug a garden to her strummed guitar
"I entered upon the busy stage of life
with ideas which had they been true
would have made this Earth a paradise
dreams of youth unpoisoned by ambition
my angel Mother kind hearted father
my first standards of human nature
wealth was not the incentive led me here
Ambition kindled its fires in my breast
but the flame was a mild and gentle one
consisting more of the wish to build up
the others' fortunes and happiness
asylum for sufferers from selfish avarice
the mania for speculation
and you my friend
how shall I ever thank you enough
for venturing into this wilderness
how express the happiness
of the ten days visit
Gardens and rosy bowers
and ever verdant groves

music books and intellectual amusements
can all be ours
Millions could not buy them
but the right disposition with competence
insures them"
his words intended for María too
spoken as well of whoever endured
a shameless poet as Lonn Taylor did
as the days turned to weeks & months
of shaving & bathing & listening to
his recording of a Prokofiev ballet
the *Cinderella* foretold Elisa's *plié*
chimed a warning it was time to go
Lonn's classical collection surprising so
even more his mind on hearing that drawl
his by far the deepest guttural
a snorting infectious high-pitched laugh
no idle claim of "nowhere but Texas"
by the case consumed bock Shiner beer
knew state politics Schulenberg to Freer
could speak to meaning of a post-oak fence
Virginia worm zig-zag split-rail stake & rider
each "impervious to cattle hogs or high winds"
"a more handsome ornament than the chain-link"
suddenly his booming voice turning sentimental
as he'd plead with Leslie to go for a pitcher
at Scholz Garten before they would close
when her text of *Child Psych* fell to the floor
then squeezed as a threesome in his VW Bug
was she who mentioned the book by Griffith
her ex-teacher on a Dickinson under duress
its *Long Shadow* cast for all these years
her own too who saw to it others got through
lent moral support before that call to Chile

& after when it came to making a choice
had set her love life aside to listen & serve
a Sacajawea had guided safely across
yet what solace will these memories be
to survivors changed from young & cocky
so certain the plans would all work out
a re-run of collisions have mostly outlived
in some ways turned out for the better
& if for the worse will retracing a stream
reverse where waters ran out of control
in a blind moment dragged so quickly down
with the rudder gone why recover an oar
in remembrance will a river ever renew itself
in holding onto it won't it just grow stagnant
no answers to give just this lifted footage
this overflow of gratitude goes on & on

San Gabriel

San Gabriel

with the north fork out of its banks
as it pushed & gushed to gain the Gulf
felt another flood of past impressions
gathering force from this final street
swept up in all had branched out from it

crossing the highway's concrete bridge
saw in the rushing & raging below
broken limbs & the tops of trees
ragweed tips & the Johnson grass
grown tall along this river's edge

swaying in the relentless swollen wind
of waters beyond the depth of any
María there at home awaiting word
had gotten through   had made it safely
so fearful after days of unceasing rain

with engines stalled & drivers trapped
then washed away   only caught up in
thrown off by all there was to sing
carried by memories beyond her reach
of years spent here before she came

men & women suddenly gone forever
in Shoal Creek's unimagined torrent
beneath the Colorado's deceptive calm
so happy to have her there to worry
not for the hurt it would give to her

but to know her care still coursing
in veins as in those vows exchanged
after finding her on her far-off shores
on becoming with her a more than one

from a wedding set by routes & trails

by passages taken over sands & seas
by the endless caravans & caravels
of all those pioneers & conquistadors
a continent apart then brought together
though on this day had gone alone

past the systems plant of IBM
183 entrance to Texas Instruments
condominiums & shopping centers
suburbs once their hunting grounds
paved parking lots their cedar hills

family around them & plentiful fruit
with the garrison facing the hostile side
as defense against the dreaded Apache
the missions built for bringing them in
with irrigation from its delicious stream

the tribes in their "natural inconstancy"
drawn off dependably years at a time
by an occult power no Padre divined
awaited each day the children's return
Hierbipiame Mayeye Deadose Yojuane

came again though never for long
their destroyers not the enemy Lipan
but rather the Fathers' measles & pox
meaning to save them yet in the end
sent them down to complete defeat

river where buffalo & Tonkawa roamed
first named for Xavier   one more saint

by those had it most in mind to change
the religious course of their native life
by turning into fertile their arid lands

Ranchería Grande received the Word
from Spain's official King & Queen
along with fanegas of chilis & beans
every 12 or 15 days a butchered bull
only feeling blessed with bellies full

"luxuries are inventions or phantasms
we can invent and give reins to fancy
in Texas as well as anywhere else"
his vision reaching to Brushy Creek
though no sign of their coming back

on through Lampasas   San Saba   Brady
to a desolate town called somehow Eden
where stopped the Volks at its chain café
where the single waitress taking orders
on being asked to change a dollar

gave back the least celestial look
then phoned ahead to San Angelo
another town christened by Catholic faith
served the deep needs of all among
the earliest to come from Mexico

from that paradise calling Gerald Lacy
to say would be delayed in getting in
jested that spot was hard to leave
though never deny the magnetism
the long tug of a people & place

ever in the native's heart & mind
just as this river enraged in spring
will erode with unreasoning allure
torn at forever by town after town
pecan groves & orchards of peach

by plowed fields on treeless plains
stretching flat under Caprock skies
taken in as if some dream come true
a love affair not even a criminal past
any present wrongs can quite undo

recall from Fort Concho in the 1880s
a buffalo soldier at McDonald's saloon
a Black private there danced for drinks
a San Saban telling him Don't you stop
unarmed trooper did & sheep man shot

"indicted for murder in the first degree
... transferred for trial to Austin
the jurors had scarcely left their seats
before they'd brought the verdict in: not guilty
and the 'matter passed into history'"

would not make this another such job
nor one advised by an Army surgeon
"the privies attached to the barracks
should be white-washed & disinfected
the slop barrels with Carbolic acid"

look back now to the form it's taken
Satan surveys his troops in their fall
remember this street of river's name
at times its heaven a more than hell

a pained awareness of the little given

in uniform on review can feel it chafe
can hear Mary's letter dated 8th of June
heartily sick of the old world's doings
tyrannies great & small   their cruelties
fill her with abhorrence of self & species

prays he firmly oppose all servitude
longs so for the peace of a simple life
"will admit no debasing passions"
no longer to seek for overmuch
will not then be so disappointed

in writing of retiring & settling down
he fears being even in spite of himself
"borne along on the course of events
into a stormy and troubled sea
the past is but a picture

a shadow of various hues   the future
we know not what   theological and myth-
ological contradictions   inconsistencies
make it everything anything nothing"
then hears again her injunction

"'laugh away care' . . . Adiós amiga mía"
& again ten days hence
in "a melancholy void"
she he says "must fill it"
sees them together out on ponies

scampering down to the beach
over & across the flowering prairies

to a green carpet the woods infringe
beside the water's wide expanse
friendship   happiness   but then

letting "that chord alone"
switches to economy & plainness
to "Heaven help us from extremes"
"keep in view the dark as well as the bright
if disappointment come it then will be

deprived of a part of its sting"
& after Valentines the taciturn man
grown loquacious in writing again
is fond & frank & signs himself
with "a long farewell"

but where did it all begin
for a start have pinned it down
to San Gabriel Street & that rented room
yet how many others for reaching there
& beyond to all can barely measure

in '33 Mary saying of a Brazos branch
"salt enough to pickle pork
never overflows its banks" but then in '34
its mouth obstructed by a narrow bar
the kind can always form from sand

lost it all   cattle & corn
& before that flood raging cholera
set them back by some seven years
here by the bills & the children ill
excuses when little or nothing came

thrown off course by divergent views
cowed by events might misrepresent
feared discount the thinnest tributary
north at Amon Carter's old Fort Worth
May Street's last full block at Berry

its tales told in sketches left unfinished
of each house with its own to tell
Grandad's three for wife & daughters
the middle one bought by Alvin & Sis
from uptown moved the grandest for Nan

from Throckmorton near Standard Printing
Mother & Dad's shop in '40 before the war
when big outfits forced them out of business
put to sleep there with teddy on a paper bin
at that rented house fed cards in a tiny press

from its backyard flew missions 'round the globe
dials & controls on apple crate crayon-drawn
grounded for taking off before the nap
for setting a match to the railway's right-of-way
smoke signals read by firemen doused the blaze

with tonsils removed returned to those rooms
where Mother half sick from the ether urped
a Shetland pony Daddy paid for never arrived
tuned in there to Sky King & ordered his ring
glowed in the dark & contained a secret code

on Nan's corner lot waded her double pond
where goldfish swam under water-lily pads
her patio with its redwood monkey works
Kung Fu statue between two sticky cypress

Austin: a Poem

his speech of water off his cast-iron tongue

by dawn she had pulled the moss & weeds
stoked her black potbelly wood-burning stove
baked canned biscuits would dip in butter
fresh pecans sizzling in melted brown sugar
the incense of her cooking in the morning air

while across the street at Terry Timmons' home
Kimbrough set her dial for the Breakfast Club
marched with Don McNeil 'round the dining table
his Granny with napkined Coke or a Dr. Pepper
needed with George & Annie Ruth gone to Jesus

his Uncle Jimmy then couldn't hold a job
thrilled to hear his vivid lies of Pacific isles
he as an Audie Murphy behind enemy lines
capturing singlehanded a machine-gun nest
Argonne forest heroics boys clamored for

not neighbor girls who knew horses & sex
those climbed after in Nan's sprawling vitex
fought with one day   made up the next
games all began with choosing of sides
chased them till nightfall when all called in

the hide & seek of their tanned aroma
puzzled by how they could differ so
at Halloween threw the spookiest parties
led blindfolded then by their softer hands
to feel wet grapes they said were eyeballs

even María seen by the light of their lamp
recognized later by those sights & sounds

before she had stitched her tapestried past
before Ovalle first heard her mandolin voice
her photo developed in that alchemical wash

armies bought on Hemphill at the five-&-ten
in mask & costume turned pirate or goblin
nickel-&-dime dreams unawakened from
White Theater stars yet showing the way
buses boarded to ad posters stay & stay

their Don't Get Off still ringing in ears
with each day another drop or a trickle
a deeper immersion in the poem to be
all the rills collected to a roaring river
poured southward here to Estevan's city

rivulets forking or joining once more
then here at San Gabriel to touch within
the miracle of how in any man may flow
the brooks of when & wherever he's been
points north or south though never to meet

met in the meaning of the memory stream
as out of South Texas sand & prickly pear
came again that summer from Hebbronville
carrying within Cowtown's Trinity River
its zoo miniature train & its Ferris wheel

two doors down from 19th to house them all
where lived as well with those ships at port
tankers dribbling rust in the Neches bend
driven by on workdays at Spector's store
his Guarantee Shoes by the tracks on Pearl

fit feet from every walk of Beaumont life
all keeping company down this final street
its namesake the same south-flowing river
brings back that summer returned to rent
from Bill Faulkner Dave Hickey's friend

who managed that San Gabriel apartment
& edited *Triad* too fine literary magazine
earlier had come there to submit to Dave
as *Riata* editor a piece on Gertrude Stein
accepted for '63's Lost Generation issue

then from that time & that rented room
the writing had begun to spill & spray
as if from out of some biblical rock
sent from there drifting down by Dave
to marking the seeming miles of essays

& through that address introduced too
to Debabrata Ghosh lived 3 blocks north
geneticist vegetarian & a fan of Tagore
would hit him up for return trip to Chile
with its denouement of an awkward kiss

& what would Estevan's reaction have been
as an opponent of the "mania for speculation"
how approve such a loan toward puppy love
the taking a chance with Ghosh's hundred
another from Popo & three from Alums

would outright lie for the largest chunk
when an agency reported no credit rating
no bank about to fund any venture south
but with Dacy's conspicuous deposit pouch

talked big business   a tall investment tale

an Indian researcher a Roma teacher-rancher
ex-students enamored of rampant Longhorns
a loan officer's finance of a mushy romance
those footed the fare through Panama City
to a landing in Lima a letdown at Cerrillos

Santiago's airport reunion had shelled out for
disappointed after months of dreaming it there
found the scheme a failure the Garden cursed
could hear them all repeating   Told you so
with their money gone for a bubble burst

their investment lost on a pair unsuited
discovered on train with her to Puntiagudo
in her Citroneta to Quillota & Viña del Mar
high interest paid for the finding there
a difference as between Pacific & Andes

her family *fundo* with its brand of cheese
a silver bell tinkled for the Mapuche maids
taught them the use of their sewing machine
lived out back somewhere behind the kitchen
with hands red from serving hers softly gloved

"agriculture cattle raising and other labors
to which they're dedicated could not be carried on
without the aid of the robust and indefatigable arms
of that race of the human species
who to their misfortune suffer slavery"

yet then to prove a serendipitous trip
as all the anguish & bitter regret

Austin: a Poem

would gain returns so unexpected
directed as though by a destiny led
to María's modest home on Pyramid

welcomed there with open arms
even taken in weak with vermin
her sister cooking the curative meals
her nanny washing the plates & sheets
& Beauty giving up her place to sleep

later on to repay all those loans in full
to the banker Exes & trusting friends
earning for a debtor greatest dividends
made possible first by a startling knock
at that San Gabriel apartment at 1 a.m.

on opening the door & standing in shorts
saw Bill McReynolds who brought the news
had been chosen to follow in Hickey's steps
the mantle passed or the proverbial buck
trembled with joy shook with thinking ahead

when before had wandered in a morbid frame
ups & downs of numbered & river streets
pacing unsurely past their fragrant blooms
in search of a flowering might correspond
lend relief from a withering shriveling mind

found it for a while at that rooming house
905 West 22nd among those friends of Louis
his closest an Indian failed his prelims twice
others taught Hindustani at meatless meals
to fix them a ritual always began with rice

observed until at Lupe's Spanish Village
learned refried beans strictly forbidden
since cooked in a prohibited animal fat
craved once again that indigenous diet
a strength it gave not alone ingredients

in that gabled house in Lou's one room
he'd read again Dickens' *Edwin Drood*
cribbed there from him to fear no prose
yet never to praise that story he wrote
of a Scotsman wedded to an octoroon

or another printed in *Corral* for '63
of a lonely figure his spitting image
an office worker in a dry goods store
too shy to approach the cute salesgirl
sends to her from the balcony above

customers' change in a metal cylinder
unseen & self-despised in spying on her
finds in his mirror at night a deep façade
so hating then each dreary weekend
doing reserve duty at camp in Killeen

a better writer than had admitted to him
out of jealousy or have his words & themes
with time improved matured & come to
after all these years on finding it takes
far more than ever supposed it would

as Estevan's story has gained with age
hired out to work in those mines of lead
so determined to pay off all of his debts
the one for Butler's Arkansas slaves

"harassed him more than any event"

liabilities to Louis & his Hindi friends
had not confessed how deep they went
& worse having usurped them from him
who in loneliness had needed them so
how in the world make it up to him

compounded more with each return
& in front of Burns blind from birth
necking with Andrea wore his ring
as Estevan declared "a cruel affair
have never known so base a man"

fissures open where seemingly safe
limestone resting on pre-cretaceous
properly belongs to Potomac series
approaches San Gabriel St. at 28th
jointed fractured weathered but there

& then at 24th will abruptly stop
but don't be fooled since it reappears
at 22nd just above in a blue clay bluff
downhill then to Fort Worth limestone
at Pease Park where a cork would pop

Jim's champagne toast to getting engaged
his marriage later flat as an opened bottle
both after scratching beneath the surface
to discover an instinct for survival apart
predatory as shark teeth in another clay

like those show up in the Eagle Ford
along with a last outcrop of *Exogyra*

arietina's greenish tint as it exposes
a greater diversity of chalky deposits
than in any other area of equal extent

at Lamar in that science received a D
to repeat it here only to start & drop
blamed that indifferent lab instructor
marked off for a misspelled pteropod
he himself had to use the textbook for

slid down Shoal Creek "slippery as soap"
in dress pants so expensive to dry-clean
in a pasture's mud slopped to Pilot Knob
to a submarine volcano as classes before
resentful of that search for long explored

preferred to excavate the strata of friends
found alone or in composite each unique
with their feldspathic & pyroxene blends
destined like a species to become extinct
now attempt for each a lasting pentastich

wanted from the first to trace their ways
in the geology of a dynamic present day
repudiated fossil fates had to memorize
would retain the vitality of a living line
revealing the record of each Texan life

later on re-reading that course's lessons
uncovered their crystalline selves intact
under pressure of their compacted pasts
struck in embedded layers phrases of
a pyrite assayed proved highest grade

with paltry nuggets any stanza contains
metamorphosed not by shearing a fault
but magma mingled with reason's cold
a cooling of passion for deceptive gold
feelings solidified by that time & place

first sensed at 1906 of this river street
though forms no part of Waller's map
as first mayor of city had laid the plat
yet for so long & fully has figured in
while hastening here there to or from

as too on that same west-campus side
where rented those garage apartments
on Poplar St. behind Alpha Epsilon Pi
where "hey Bernie throw me the ball"
is a yell can still hear hanging on high

at both addresses remember once more
the debts remain to named & unnamed
Morton with fine heart-warming humor
Jim with his visual pun on prickly pear
has drawn readers to a poetry of others

knew Andy on Poplar as never before
sketched by Jon when sat for him there
fell out with George & the Science Org
heard red-head David practice on violin
foretold Bach's partitas & Darío's bow

Morton then rooming just across 19th
when shared his taste for bottled brew
& for jazz solos from the Golden Age
Bix's cornet his piano on "In a Mist"

NORK Red Nichols the amazing Miff

"the foursquare same-way-every-time
ragtime feel" of the ODJB's '17 style
Dutrey   Kid Ory   & Vernon's own
trombonists all in a Twenties' tradition
whose licks he imitated to keep it alive

born in Teagarden's stomping grounds
& like Big T born too to travel around
to leave Wichita Falls for eastern roots
though then after quarts he'd introduce
his pride in this place's western twang

at Shakey's Pizza Parlor dixied nights
at 29th & Guadalupe his old-time tone
& straight-ahead drive reviving a need
to play it "For No Reason at All in C"
but to rhythm & rhyme Estevan's city

when frats laughed for cuddliest dates
howled & guffawed at Chaplin's tramp
Morton would find it deeply offensive
an affront to comedy he so dearly loved
"nothing" he'd say "can be that funny"

knowing too well the sadness beneath
his own covered up by Mercutian wit
would clasp both hands upon his chest
breathe deeply & release a heaviest sigh
Norma Shearer kissing his poisoned lips

visiting later in Hobbs on Yeso Street
forgot his French horn behind the car

backed out & crumpled its costly bell
yet took it with a comic's stoic poise
his remake of a Laurel & Hardy flick

listened with him in an ell-shaped room
where on a weekend "Spillway" written
Riata logo coming in a morning dream
from Anheuser-Busch label's eagled A
on the bottles would together consume

as after awaking conceived that cover
with rather a rattler curled about an R
& cactus in a southwestern landscape
above it a sunset spreading orient rays
but needed an artist could render it all

so across campus to find Ralph White
a full-professor in Department of Art
its far-off building not entered before
with turpentine- & paint-fumed halls
easels with nudes in charcoals & oils

he to send for Jim few students knew
in his vintage DeSoto going with him
to the Tavern on 12th St. to have a few
discuss that design had come to mind
then discovered in him the one & only

warm bright & eager & from Amarillo
poor & working his way through school
renting then off Blanco right up the hill
across from the old Military Institute
a one-room once a blacksmith's shop

proved a training ground for making do
where the endless arguments all began
over deadlines & each's differing view
he at the drawing board night after night
bent there with always his twitching eye

those bare rock walls & roof beams
reeked of smoke & of dampened ash
though rarely if ever his fireplace lit
food barely afforded much less wood
while his own brain a glowing smithy

burning three days & nights in a row
forged over & over each layout page
would pull it all up & start once more
stick iron back in & pump the bellows
hammering plunging tempering again

was driven crazy   just wanted it done
had not "checked haste urges men to mar
the dignity of every act" rushing into print
then regretting the flaws   never learning
from Dante from Estevan from patient Jim

"men of enlightened judgement
unshaken perseverance integrity of purpose
calmly put their shoulders to the wheel
toil for the good of others without their trying
to force it forward prematurely"

those who take their time
who make it serve for more
spend longer hours than most
to see the contract worded right

better placement of artwork & type

their loss of sleep another's reward
the accuracy of their selfless touch
with a craft & care can alchemize
till weeks & months have all paid off
have achieved a design wins the award

yet not without demands they make
kept awake through half those nights
crawling for the details out in the dark
aiming a flashlight & holding it steady
from buckboard wheel to his sketch pad

as if Euryalus & Nisis gone out on sortie
through Rutulian ranks so deadly to both
their enemies undone by Bacchus & dice
then delayed by cutting of a bloody swath
& weighted down with their heavy booty

caught by Volcens & the returning guards
one's neck a flower stem the mower lops
the other speared to bleed wine-red drops
on his beloved friend's so luckless corse
incomparable scene yet no dearer than this

a fraternity's yard among stinging nettles
with its Roundup party still a bash inside
its antique buggy parked out on the grass
flat on stomachs for catching the spokes
to be superimposed on a '90s' mustache

Jim's synthesis created as illustration for
Bratcher on Stephen Crane Texas stories

an essay written while his Cherokee wife
expected a child & he kept her very well
taking her fresh bouquets would be let in

to aromatic loaves of oven-baked bread
bought him his quart of whatever brand
to keep him going   & stayed with him
through his every wry & sober sentence
his paragraphs best with abundant drink

only left him acting as a pumpkin-eater
to drive with Jim to Memorial Museum
there on San Jacinto for drawing a gun
some revolver by Colt or a Remington
as one more piece in his picture puzzle

adding too other typical western motifs
like the live oak framing Stephen's face
captured for artwork's cumulative effect
along with the dry & weathered carriage
caught while frats all slapped & bragged

then locked in a tray inked & printed
for those might one day come to read
"far straight shadows in back of stars"
Crane's prose view to Grecian echoes
his no pledge class's but Sophoclean

though even so the prop was theirs
supplied a touch above the cravat
to that easterner's high stiff collar
if unconscious nevertheless survives
beyond their booze so soon wore off

can only claim the hand-punched holes
in his Asian sunburst & licked red seals
stuck on his black overlapping ribbons
paid for too from all but empty pockets
for a 2nd striking cover of Jim's design

& thanks to Bratcher earned a little extra
from tutoring swimming & diving teams
till upset him by "No Perching Allowed"
antic piece published in *The Daily Texan*
from Zukofsky's being uninvited to read

short-tempered stocky & so outspoken
could not understand that one position
though still return to his written words
his helping the athletes at every hour
his Cherokee happily inside her shell

& all integrated through meticulous Jim
a single instance yet repeated how often
like bookmarks punched for *Cow's Skull*
his tricolored ribbons trimmed & laid in
& photos for *Strangers* by Sandra Lynn

cannot complain would do it over again
though never can it be as it was back then
when it all turned out as Jim had planned
nightly fights waged on Mountain Dew
many a swig taken for making it through

only to be damned by the *Texan* letters
as a childish exorbitant Christmas tree
the whole idea of any East-West issue
a waste of every student's blanket fee

thinking then would throw in the towel

when with it out would receive that call
from Ransom's office at the Tower's base
recalls Yeats' battlements of history & myth

his peering from his ancient Gaelic pile
to where a blind man's song reveals
all hearts since Helen have been betrayed

to that of Cret's design blind Borges came
felt walls where Whitman took deadly aim
dropped Eckman's son & ten victims more

from *The Odyssey*'s circular view
Telémakhos still pondered alone
the hope held out by Athena's words

while Frank Dobie would set no store
by any such Greek erection
to him an impotent prick of imported style

saw it only as one more sign
of the finding inferior
whatever's here on ranch or range

like the dogtrot architecture cools in summer
yet before its clock struck one
stirred each Friday by its carillons

rang Brahms's variations across the Mall
or at night on exiting stadium gates
gazed up with a shameful joy

at its columnar top
glowing with orange
for victorious sports

there too so often had searched in vain
through winning football seasons from '60 on
for the smallest gains over a vast unknown

sought in the library's morgue-like catalog
a living food for a brain half starved
fingering there the stained file cards

forever hopeful   forever lost
baffled by Dewey & later the new LC
on entering those holy of holies

stacks closed to the undergrad
could take no elevator to its dim-lit floors
emblem itself of a groping start

harder before that bachelor degree
permitted an ascent upon one's own
to explore alone among the broken books

where before had had to fill a slip
to hand a request at the checkout desk
to haughty clerks looked to know it all

such deep needs searched by unseen hands
then dropped from above in their pulley box
clanked & screeched as it brought them down

volumes lowered to the sophomore
more sacred then on their showing up

Dave Oliphant

at a sliding door as though untouched

tomes ever taking much longer to read
than death-like due dates stamped in red
even getting through them not guaranteed

would discover the key
could decipher the meaning
of sentence paragraph or chapter

confounded further
made to suffer evermore
for just wanting to know

or wrote the wrong call number
saw 8 for 3
or I for T

those numbers & letters
drawn by student drones
in '61 became another cog

hired by the hour
to prepare the cloth
to print them straight & clear

so shelvers would not replace them
out of their proper order
numerical or alphabetical

& yet confusion might have aided
in passing through to the unsuspected
if learned at all ever learned too late

new publications ever considered the best
with their bindings so clean & smooth
on them the ink would adhere with ease

not so with those were old & brittle
whose authors ever seemed the same
those not assigned never looked into

pens gouging their softened spines
periods beading up on greasy leather
slick from use in a backward time

untrained in calligraphy or fixative sprays
the figures coming out too large or small
blinded the eyes in the o's & e's

others seated at their loaded trucks
mostly foreigners or majored in art
like the precise machine-like Japanese

or an Eastern European
Nowotny her name
a Dean of Students' the same

she a divorcee with a child at home
who read those early stumbling tries
told of how she picked up Spanish

by selling at night her debit policies
attended classes first then labeled on
such a bore she said but had a son to feed

little thought where that search would lead
to what way-stations

what cornices on the journey "up"

then full circle to the HRC
though returning still unlettered
even with critics all faithfully read

back to where it all began
to its rare collections   first housed them there
at the Tower's base in whispering rooms

Harry Huntt Ransom's bargain buys
books correspondence & iconography
the manuscripts galleys & page proofs

scholars & workers so cramped for space
Bracker beside a sink in a converted kitchen
cataloging the archive of Christopher Morley

mixed him up with a writer of Shakespeare's age
another error   another unknown author
then revealed by friendship with his avid fan

his verses in tribute to Dorothy Wordsworth
to a Whitman preface Hazlitt's sense of place
men who Borges admired as well

in style he & Morley Americas apart
yet one in their love of those predecessors
had first come to find another

Sir Walter with his *History of the World*
written between gazing from London's Tower
on the far-off Virginia grass

state named for her who condemned him there
the Ocean Shepherd's fickle Faery
Ralegh's own hard-hearted Scinthia

her loyal knight who penned a poem
so difficult still to enter
one mentioned by Colin in Spenser

come home again from Kilcolman
filled the library's orangey form
for his allegory of a hidden stream

in hopes somehow it might let in
unlock that courtier's imprisoned sense
in his expansive Elizabethan prose

his rolling record of earth & time
& even with his tongue enclosed in stone
perhaps by way of that virgin's land

where Estevan had first drawn breath
that poet too inhaled this cedar air
breathed more deeply with Ransom's call

all after shared that upstairs apartment
with George a friend since junior high
together in classes & in marching band
on high school speech & orchestra trips
competing & performing at tournaments

as a threesome had with Lloyd Lejeune
camped out near those muscadine vines
in a grove by Texas Gulf Sulfur's mine
off a shell-paved road ran the other way

to George's step-dad's hamburger stand

served the best ground chuck & round
cattycorner to the South Park Drive-In
a block from monument to Spindletop
a framed photo in his Beaumont home
with spout towering as a broken blade

suspended in vacant coastal sky
for more than three score years
the black ray as if of rising rain
with profits had not then fallen
unfailing as his Mom's goulash

tented in a pasture where Cubby ran
barking in circles for half the night
at noises out in the frightening dark
a crackling of sticks & brittle leaves
at dawn awakened to cattle stared in

on Fourth sold fireworks down the way
near gusher had burst & showered all
fenced-in with a marker to keep its date
shot off cherry bombs had thought to rival
a Boom meant mammon's almighty dollar

deaf then to all the jobs it brought
knew it more as that favorite spot
littered with Trojans parkers tossed
engaged then more in religious love
snubbed those after the bods & bucks

lacked any notion of what it was worth
how its pumps had piped checks to pay

for Estevan's beloved language school
its tenured professors damned to death
all but idolized in the very same breath

how rigs had plunged the diamond bits
for fueling a tribute Barker would build
to honor Estevan's "thorough greatness"
papers Bugbee secured through R.L. Batts
for study with Southern Fund of Littlefield

that George a Major left long-term notes
with interest for collecting a wrongful past
had outdrawn a hired gun in the Civil War
spared a druggist who had hoarded liquor
said Ferguson firing Battle a big mistake

at polling booths would pay out silver
for every proper Negro vote
shipping the beef north & east
to him sheer folly since soon the State
would buy it back in imported steaks

the later George not after a fortune
just bred thoroughbreds in Arkansas
taught till divorce & then re-upped
when stationed in Korea near DMZ
cooked in Palestine mother's recipes

tried something new most every week
the latest gear gimmick fad or trick
quickly thereafter grew tired of each
a computer watch played Sinclair's "Eyes"
an acetylene cannon scared Andy shitless

happened when he rode in South Park days
in George's '52 Henry J with Jimmy Hayes
who had hid in front underneath their seats
that harmless flame-throwing mechanism
aimed it so it roared & blazed at his feet

would show off gadgets found or bought
anything to amaze friends or adversaries
in early teens passed the hardest exams
first in his class had his driver's license
first to be licensed to operate as a ham

though known most as a practical joker
never laughed at his hometown's name
Goose Creek beneath a coat of varnish
on a '30s souvenir his uncle picked up
always so proud of where he was born

but thought it strange he took to heart
that long-ago phone company's photo
of a building-shack he had never seen
yet a call to something so deep within
would only come out on Poplar Street

that part of him proved an untapped well
blown in by a bitter nitroglycerin dispute
a debate so unlike the forensic speeches
he had prepared for his & Jimmy's team
when were given topics so meaningless

Should farmers be paid not to plant
Should a nuclear freeze begin or cease
What's the safest way to make world peace
In education which should it be

More science math or humanities

little to do with a preference test
when the candidates first squared off
to him Nixon had had the upper hand
knew what to say had a superior style
could keep Kennedy for all he cared

even so in a way sort of like that choice
a fireworks display over the real or fake
setting off those loud pain-giving cracks
loaded words exploded in sensitive ears
in each other's darkened hardening face

in that tiff was even defending him
by attacking his friends attended Org
swore their testimonies were insincere
while he would stand up for all of them
then moved out & rented a single room

off Nueces down from Barkley Arms
a rooming house with its hotel awning
its polished brass an art major dubbed
"The Armpit" & painted it onto a sign
faced towards Dirty's hamburger joint

widowed Mrs. Ninks its blind landlady
whose roof & second floor rotted away
one boarder even stepped right through
she listened close for the stairs to creak
as a student would sneak out not to pay

later on to learn of his Science group
he had never meant so much to them

no religion measured up to friendship
or the bivouac shared near Spindletop
the hopes & doubts after double dates

Estevan too came to hold that view
even to believe the clergy enslaved
oppressed through dumb obedience
he opposing such corrupt influence
a fanaticism defying common sense

but saw his colonists bound by law
to profess at least the Catholic faith
to marry by authority of holy church
then welcomed as a friend Muldoon
for in "Paddy" he found a liberal wit

an unwed Father who like himself
"looked to Texas as his only home"
his "resting place" & on applying
for 11 leagues confirmed his belief
in that vain benevolent Irish priest

who would as colonist Bill Rabb had
perform the one service Estevan held
devotes a man to wherever he lands
to his giving of more & craving less
on inhabiting a property invested in

with Paddy led to touch his earth
shout aloud for letting it echo him
setting stakes to mark deep within
pull its herbs & throw its stones
taking sweet & bitter into bones

Austin: a Poem

& though he would later come to sell
his deeds there outlive his ownership
for from that soil his rhyming thrived
the words he had written surviving still
"The zigzag dart! th' astounding crash!"

"luscious views that expand the heart"
chose the homemade over plagiarism
native flora before any foreign type
prayed that "religious discord fall
And friendship be the creed of all"

& would never fail to visit those
jailed in Mexico or in Matamoros
by the cruel & jealous of any day
a Gómez Farías of violent means
who threw Wharton in a dungeon

when then Paddy did not hesitate
to use his office to arrange escape
deception through his cleric's robe
a cassock the Padre had smuggled in
consecrated cloth outwitting a guard

George too to appear a deliverer of sorts
when in Ft. Worth after had broken it off
her parents declaring should see a shrink
from the letter written & ring redeemed
taken then by him to his Arkansas hills

neutral grounds of Caddo & Quahpaw
carried the sick & wounded by travois
to the foot of Ozarks' curative springs
a million gallons daily at 143 degrees

he filling troughs with water & feed

with dam unwilling stud indiscriminately
spilling his seed as he'd talk of breeding
of thinking to quit teaching public school
to move to Fayetteville for an MA degree
major in communications minor in speech

this soon after his first Nancy proved
unable to bear with his unsettled ways
later to meet & wed his Georgia peach
a Cracker to some though none to him
a brain in her class had married young

been deserted just as George arrived
her son adopted & their own to come
then shipped overseas on a tour of duty
to train on cabbage for "the gentle way"
return with a black belt his master gave

take his family to the Palestine pines
through distance & crisis still in touch
roommates ever by the ties that bind
by rockets yet flare & a dog barks on
the errors accepted & the juries hung

a cement holds from that garage apartment
true as well through difference with Andy
patched up by hearing a Scherchen Mahler
listened there together to scherzo & ländler
cut classes for symphonies far more urgent

& equally for Count Basie's "Lil' Darlin'"
atomic album with Lockjaw tenor screams

detonated over & over off its upstairs walls
when the opening chords on Green's guitar
would set heads straighter than any lecture

Black music for putting a spirit back in
thought history had taken it out of them
by then having done its very damnedest
yet there they were on & for the record
could enliven not lease a Poplar apartment

at the Co-op to find a first Ornette Coleman
on "Congeniality" his white plastic alto sax
as if moaning "I'm Goin' tooo Foat Wuth"
in the Union to catch Bobby Bradford live
those both getting back to Cowtown scales

in between on weekends cleaned up the place
when Andy would prepare a bohemian meal
wine & candlelight imitating a Puccini scene
celebrated his new piece for celeste & strings
& to buy for the occasion a button-down shirt

would buy one too not to do the laundry
too busy composing to bother with Duz
the brighter his ideas the later at night
slept till noon through that major quiz
hoping absence would somehow wash

the important thing his composition
professors mostly stick-in-the-muds
had gone on repeating or given it up
from those would learn their lesson
even if flunked would not succumb

from its chest of drawers "Order of Worship"
out its bedroom window "this is just to say"
just two verses from that vital time & place
the latter printed in Bracker's *Penny Poems*
reviewed by Eckman in the college's paper

but did not think then of weaving together
a long poem made from a one-block street
so persuaded was only going nowhere fast
nothing could come of any Texan no ways
unaware Barker had written a block away

had Andy to reassure   though not for long
German survived through the summer & fall
yet failed required Government departmental
& while he exempt from a childhood asthma
was classified 1-A at pre-induction physical

dropped out in dread of draft board greetings
would go east before they arrived in the mail
would meet up in NYC & travel on to Philly
where he studied then with Rochberg at Penn
& recorded for Nonesuch his electronic flaws

"Hubris" most impressive of the tragic four
its bassless notes whirring higher & higher
till its faint tinkle dissipates then disappears
sounds so unheard in that shared apartment
though the same as those in nourishing still

felt pride in one another in spite of dissent
ever wanting to avoid any pent-up critique
no sooner expressed than regretted at once
after honest remarks an argument resolved

on visiting later here or there left it unsaid

ever impatiently awaiting a letter to come
response to a latest love or to finding none
the strain of being stuck in some rotten job
mostly from growing to feel useless & low
with music or a poem completely ignored

if listened to disliked or condescended
rejected by those in a position to know
made worse when a friend depended on
would fail to reply by the expected time
cut by the slightest unsympathetic tone

though still those semesters hold the line
deliver their mutual remembered message
an assurance spoken in the intimate voice
of long-ago sessions held morning & night
convincing yet through setback or disregard

from Philly each would take a separate way
he to compose in NYC for Nikolai's troupe
to put up with talented Ray's nutty routines
rebuked when before shared humor & dance
Reck abusive & Jordan keeping his distance

when in earlier years with the two of them
he had formed their Texas Viennese Three
brought back polyrhythms & ragtime tunes
answered at last Ives' quarter-tone question
as to how daily sounds lend musical speech

while back east this accent just heard as hick
meant misunderstood   meant nothing doing

could find no work   not even as shoe clerk
ate six bananas with water in order to enlist
to pass needed three more pounds so didn't

returned then to face the inescapable fate
to impatience with the interminable wait
until when it came on that Juneteenth day
seemed against a conscript to discriminate
as if exacting in full for that same mistake

"after 200 years' occupation of similar soils
by a free-laboring community" Olmsted wrote
he had never seen "such evidence of waste
as in Texas after 10 years of slavery
How then does it continue?

by constantly borrowing & never paying its debts
the profit of slave labor only obtained
by filching from the nation's capital
from that which the nation owes its posterity
with prohibition would have prospered more rapidly"

back in Beaumont put on a bus for Houston
there in a line told Turn your head & cough
when only after insisting their oracle scales
could interpret the case of this underweight
did the *deus ex machina* officer emancipate

después with endearing wit María declaring
"Too bad really"   to her had missed out on
reveille   KP duty   being ordered around
had made a big difference done lotsa good
"Might not have turned out *tan regalón*"

then enrolled at Lamar Tech to finish at last
with hurdles cleared with Hagelman's help
beating out Beeson for the Weinbaum prize
glad & yet by his entry far more impressed
manly & direct & besides it ground an axe

would travel with him to Albuquerque & back
& rent on University Ave from June to August
checking Placement Center files in Sutton Hall
for a last-minute high-school teaching position
at interview hired for English in Hebbronville

roomed with Popo played tennis with Huerta
to hear those *Latinos* & to imbibe their words
in endless disagreement as to what they were
Indian Mexican Hispanic full-blooded Texan
called by them the Beaumont wetback gringo

rode weekends to border in perpetual motion
unending drink for Gulf cannot be quenched
stands not nor stops for the national or alien
carrying all before it preferring neither side
bearing both along by its indifferent waters

from Popo's Laredo home went to Nuevo
for *flautas* & the *Coronas* at dime a bottle
to Mandy's kitchen brought *cajeta* in jars
through sand & mesquite the gas & cattle
so-called wastelands grow special people

in November stunned in an afternoon class
by announcement on school's loudspeaker
Fort Worth boy loathing Dallas even more
that first ballot cast & still means the most

felt the bullets ripped him to void that vote

down the road to learn Oswald too attended
George C. Clarke & read too of Dick & Jane
in that Cowtown elementary sat pen in hand
in a same wooden seat with ink-well's stain
on its playground he too picked for kickball

in Zapruder movie through all the smoke
made out shots from that raised manhole
others fired nearby from the grassy knoll
felt ill cheated feared Penn Jones' theory
with even LBJ in on that vast conspiracy

cover-up so pervasive left none untouched
all caught up in the spider web of suspicion
thoughts infected by all he might have been
his refreshing face & vigorous cresting hair
Milton quote in crisis "only stand and wait"

though put off at times by his eastern talk
would hear it now in that heaviest brogue
"Ich bin" in Boston-Irish at the Berlin wall
where divisions patrolled with deadly stare
their weapons ever repeating Just you dare

his Peace Corp goes hardly anywhere now
with even plumbing lessons grown suspect
another capitalist trick to sell some fixtures
the in-fighting continuing after all the tears
from a speech moved so many to volunteer

with spring found a student young & mature
lost her but grew closer to Chicano teachers

consoled by grilled *tripa* wrapped in tortillas
by *Los cuates y Guajalote* three sophomores
by golf with Jungman a principal firm & fair

then with June came again to Estevan's city
with a bit of the language he learned so well
here to let that seminal room on San Gabriel
two doors down from Bill was about to wed
his Gloria a New Braunfels girl born & bred

her Conroe *Schatzie* a carbon copy of George
neither ever satisfied with whatever they were
two idealists would feel out of place wherever
George going from judo to a word processor
to the Bayou City's downtown archery trail

forest land set aside by Jim Hogg's daughter
preserved by Ima for each generation to come
at Batts Hall that pot-bellied Governor's statue
Rusk typesetter shot in back after took the fight
to corporate lobby a railroad trust the lynch law

fed up with administrators Bill on coming home
a mad Odysseus   George bending a stiffest bow
to surprise of Phaiákians overthrowing them all
their wives asked to move at a moment's notice
one from Palestine to Houston then back again

the other back & forth from Conroe to Austin
Bill hiking the Rockies Guadalupe Big Bend
Gloria along or alone embroidering at home
Nancy letting out pants or taking them in
Penelopes add fitting parts to a city's poem

in '69 in Albuquerque at the decade's close
the Federal case came on for a final hearing
Bill writing "Notice from last week's paper
your name is in the headlines again
Interesting how you maintain

an ambivalent sort of notoriety
Yep, your mug shot made it all the way
to Austin and its daily butt wipe
Seems as though you wrote a letter
critical of the glorious legislature

You realize, of course, that your crime
was not in writing the letter
but in getting it published
I'm writing to tell you how proud I am
Didn't know you still had it in you!

Noticed in the picture that you had
some law books under your arm Could it mean
you're defending yourself in court?
If you are, remember what Abe Lincoln said
of a man who defends himself—he's a fool

but you already knew that about yourself
One reason your situation caught my attention
was that similar things are happening around here
A teacher was fired from Del Valle High School
where Gloria teaches, because he wore a mustache

and didn't wear the right kind of clothes
A visiting speaker to a class in the same school
wasn't allowed to speak because he had long hair
The Land Commissioner ejaculated an edict

that no one who worked for the Land Commission

could wear a skirt higher than the knees
or males wear their sideburns lower
than the top of their earlobe
We lost a city council election to a bunch of
red-necks and ultra-conservatives due to a stupid,

reactionary vote   My God—what's happening?
It's almost as though we're into another McCarthy era
Are we all to lose our rights as citizens
if we don't agree with the so-called establishment?
I'll go to jail first!!!   Gloria sends her greetings to Maria

Hope your kid is alright and doesn't look like you
Maybe we'll see you in Austin sooner now
It's still a pretty town that's worth fighting for
and God knows we need the help   Even poets might
come in handy   So come on back to Texas and prove

that the pen is mightier than the dollar bill
—oops, I mean sword   P.S. Forgot to mention
the guy drove his car at 60 mph through a street
party of hippies   He courteously stopped
and backed over a few more"

in '65 with Gloria expecting Rebecca
they had rented here on this very street
just two blocks south of Barker's home
three from Beast's last cockroach stand
faced Federation Club & Neill-Cochran

in '64 Bill lived on it at 22nd near Slate
Joe a professor never published a book

just essays from his exceptional slants
on WCW or Keaton's *What! No Beer?*
dealt with students on an equal footing

listening & learning from what they read
in his taste & appetite ranging far & wide
from realms of writing to the silver screen
of food served in an Alfred Hitchcock film
on a grape-leaf casserole or French cuisine

& had found in his Patricia the perfect cook
no slipped disc held his Philadelphian back
would go with him in a cavern or to a beach
her recipes for eggs benedict pastry or bread
satisfying both his Sweetish & wisdom teeth

had only heard after rooming on San Gabriel
how he woke to two students fencing outside
going at it in the corner lamp's circle of light
at 2 a.m. their clashing foils humorous to him
as funny as his landlady Ella Pfluger Pfenning

she disturbed by Whitbread rooming out back
turning up the volume on his operas full blast
subleased & wrote "Low" Joe's favorite poem
both living then across from Faulkner & Hall
the latter a history professor would give no A

to Seals whose average had earned the grade
but told John he wasn't ready to receive it yet
next semester he wanted him back in his class
at first was infuriated & deeply resentful
but after signing up came away changed

by Silber too who sent a student of Joe's
to East Side Austin on a term assignment
gave him credit for her introduction to life
the one man Joe knew who could ever think
being born one-armed a distinct advantage

all coming together on this last river street
a directory of names gave directions taken
upset by their attitudes either for or against
by a dictatorial domination or intimidation
made angry bitter indignant until outgrown

there at the other end at twenty-six hundred
at sudden drop-off to pecans & Shoal Creek
right-angle to Poplar where two streets meet
passed Eugene's rock home unready to read
his *Life* of Estevan might have given a lead

equally Barker's own an example to follow
in '94 on failing the English entrance exam
returned to Palestine & its blacksmith shop
to hammer on its anvil in that railroad forge
to cram grammar nights with Shirley Green

then in '95 would take a train & try it again
& making it through for freshman schedule
took physics Greek German English French
by '57 all but forgotten till biographer Pool
paid him a visit & as they walked to his car

Barker to put around him a grateful arm
& thanking him for being so thoughtful
said none of his students came anymore
could have gone there in half a minute

oh to think how it might have been so

to have met his first or his last seminar
taken notes from him who Duncalf said
"had he been an Indian had been a chief
looked like one" & Webb had seen it too
an "unconscious austerity" Eugene wore

an anonymous sophomore's frank report
gave him "Standing Bull" as a sobriquet
dressed as a Sioux wrapped in a blanket
to some he possessed no more emotion
than the wooden Indian at a cigar store

to others known as "the Great Stone Face"
"granite monolith" in those sturdy tweeds
disturb his class he would turn bright red
& yanking his intellectual horn-rims off
was next thing to the 'Frisco earthquake

would praise a productive specialist less
than a generalist "ruminative sympathetic
catholic alert industrious not too hurried
to explore inviting by-paths or to wave"
"an encouraging greeting" along the way

drove on the links a long straight ball
dealt directly & plainly with one & all
fished the Trinity River & Aransas Bay
once drew in a flounder on a simple hook
if not the first always to catch the biggest

at times mounted a hobby horse of choice
to champion all subjects as of equal worth

found the arts & sciences hopelessly lost
wandered about without guide or compass
yielding to every varying fallacious wind

indulging in "unctuous elaboration of the obvious"
"his choicest castigation silently reserved for himself"
"half saber-toothed tiger half St. Francis of Assisi"
held a gapped knife in "big rough expressive hands"
saved string for the day Japs cut off the jute supply

could have camped out to catch a glimpse
of his grim determination & keen grey eye
as he "track[ed] down a slanderer of S.F.A."
but had rented on Poplar three years too late
even arrived in time had gone unrecognized

as Estevan's fisher of facts angler of annals
oblivious of them both as in Beaumont days
on shopping Kroger shelves ever the same
where across the street on Highland Ave.
Mrs. C.W. Bingman lived benefactor to be

with her humped back & her delicate health
how suspect hers a mind so nutritious & hale
sought for her scholarship a promising senior
by the serendipity theory of a Prescott Webb
found a pitiful unread would-be poet instead

whose freshman tuition fees she gladly paid
then saw his first semester's pathetic grades
another debt surviving this side of the grave
her sacred research had performed too late
not even with a doctorate to communicate

too late to visit Barker's oak-shaded place
razed from this street the most vital of all
yet a fact has confirmed the poem's design
like Hart Crane finding Roebling had lived
in his own apartment on Columbia Heights

from there that crippled engineer able to see
the cables tuned on his harp-stringed Bridge
whose sound crosses over to unlimited keys
Eugene an open sesame to that Mexican cell
& his *Life* an entrée to Poplar & San Gabriel

Bugbee's as well & though left it unfinished
has added overtones of professors & friends
of voices resonant through streets & streams
if carried on reluctantly by a sporting Barker
asserted "I had to go on because I had started

As for myself I have always been doubtful
whether a man deserved much credit for doing
a task he wanted above all else to do
there ought to be a record to which men might turn
to realize their unpaid and unpayable obligations"

remembered his wife's weeks in a Saltillo hotel
with their screenless room & no English spoken
through his monotonous study her hardships real
to María too gave something of the measure due
"has lived with me and Austin for all these years"

Austin: a Poem

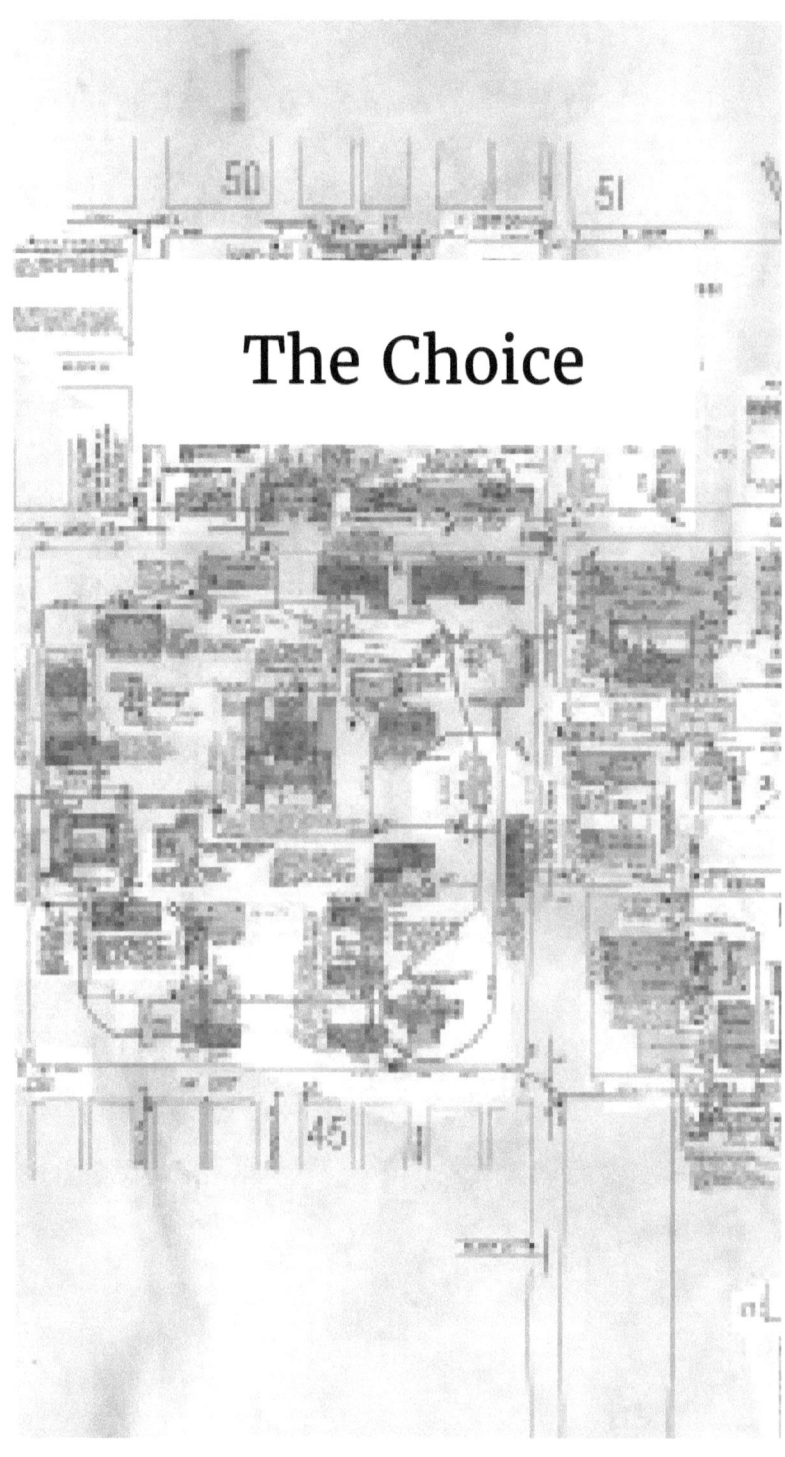

The Choice

The Choice

>after *Southwestern University 1840-1961*
>by Ralph Wood Jones

having chosen back then
not to follow in
Rev. Birkelbach's Methodist steps
now ask what if
yet with no regrets

took an easier way
a harder may be
but of the two
more likely the former
though how be sure

what might have been
had decision gone to
a life of religion
rather than the poem
if never lived unknown

this line of work
none to those who
think it simply play
not so serious as
to worship & pray

felt deeply clergy's appeal
with its selfless devotion
to the other's soul
with its readings reveal
hope's timeless universal role

yet sensed with doubts
as to tenets preached
an indifference to rituals
no vocation for one
tended so to disbelief

did not then know
how in '25 Gibbs
in order to serve
required to reply immaculate
conception yes or no

said he was certain
Christ divine & holy
God's breath had blessed
yet his application rejected
by the Convention vote

nearly a century before
horseback itinerants started west
libraries in their saddlebags
for spreading the message
Martin Ruter officially first

had come after revolution
had freed the colonists
from Mexico's Catholic law
arrived to found Societies
& their inaugural college

not a defective kind
with theater & dance
the students treated democratically
but at the will

of instructors' unworldly views

on crossing the Sabine
Martin brought his learning
where in his words
for the lack thereof
people then were perishing

his own formal schooling
ended at sixteen when
he entered the ministry
boarding with Mrs. Peckett
former housekeeper to Wesley

she sharing with Martin
her memories of John
& in her home
would loan him books
of his she owned

if only studied alone
had gained through diligence
enough of Hebrew Chaldean
Greek Latin & French
to use those languages

principal at Wesleyan Academy
president of eastern institutions
colleges Augusta & Allegheny
then Conference sent him
on his Texas mission

at 52 followed sounds
of hounds baying outside

of a smoke-filled cabin
expounded the gospel within
& above a grocery-saloon

so appalled by rule
of ignorance & vice
profanity gaming & superstition
the intemperance with which
he had to contend

yet eager to teach
& in letters home
wrote in some ways
the most beautiful place
he had ever seen

grand & enchanting prospects
vast rolling ocean-like prairies
grasses' verdure in spring
flowers spangling the green
fit for angel assemblies

of the Indians saying
had not gone further
on account of them
planned on bringing back
his family with him

a few years later
while hunting for horses
the Earthman brothers attacked
Fields escaped Henry scalped
hands lopped heart sacked

Martin as a zealot
even willing to risk
not only his life
but lives of those
he loved the most

yet in the end
on returning for them
grew sick & weary
& unable to continue
delivered his final sermon

dead before the fountain
had begun to flow
with knowledge he said
in a baccalaureate address
would never run dry

then missionary Robert Alexander
on taking Martin's place
oversaw the cornerstone laid
for his namesake College
Rutersville same as village

from it would come
schools Rev. Birk recommended:
said Attend Lon Morris
& then go on
to Southwestern & SMU

at each in turn
in Jacksonville Georgetown &
Dallas he himself matriculated
took classes in sciences

& humanities then theology

at the seminary tested
on New Testament Greek
later chaplain in war
exchanged rings with Juanita
three years his senior

Lon Morris English major
a Southwestern graduate too
from their union Ron
John & redheaded Fay
still recall each one

though more the ruddy-faced
heavy-set husband-father Elwood J.
passionate in his pulpit
in his book-lined study
accessible night & day

before the sanctuary doors
greeting & shaking hands
taking upon his shoulders
the trials & tribulations
of young & old

in their shabby parsonage
responded to constant calls
to visit the hospitals
bless birth or marriage
comfort at the funerals

back pain with insomnia
or his conviction lost

would lead to breakdown
& a smaller parish
then left the cloth

at his mystery-shrouded grave
no mention on inscription
of minister or chaplain
just his wartime years
as an Army captain

his stipulation or hers
from an abiding resentment
of the Church's treatment
yet both would enter
the Conference's Cemetery Center

could Stephen F. Austin
have ever thought Birk
just another "Methodist preacher
would do more mischief . . .
than a dozen horsethieves"

did Birk ever hear
of the '26 committee
probed his alma mater
for an alleged heresy
among its eminent faculty

of the five-man resolution
called for the resignation
of Professor Herbert Gray
taught virgin birth unessential
to teachings of Scripture

even worse his remark
on disciples had seen
Jesus walk on water:
it must have been
just an optical illusion

wonder too if Birk
read President Barcus' defense
of that professor's divergence
already fully incorporated in
their Book of Discipline

his arguing against signing
of articles of faith
not altogether agreeing with
"can be no doubt
what we Methodists believe"

declared pastors will often
cross swords on questions
of depravity of man
moral state of children
literal fire & brimstone

of the Second Coming
thought it quite impossible
to formulate a statement
would manage to receive
every pastor's hearty assent

challenged the sincerity of
acquiescence in ecclesiastical creeds
asserted glory of Methodism
her placing no restrictions

on search for truth

imprudent to his mind
for a popular body
like the Texas Conference
to pass on accuracy
of Bible or science

held the difficulty of
fixed formulas for faith
advocated at church academies
both freedom of speech
& subjects to teach

if had known then
of that resolute defender
would that have meant
a change of mind
a life so different

perhaps yet still prefer
praise for the lives
these lines would honor
the circuit riders' sacrifices
such a wise administrator

but above them all
Birk the spiritual intellectual
inspired that unanswered call
became instead one craves
this service also saves

About Dave Oliphant

Born in Fort Worth, Texas, in 1939, **Dave Oliphant** taught and/or edited a scholarly journal at The University of Texas at Austin from 1976 to 2006. In 2015, Wings Press published Oliphant's *Generations of Texas Poets*, a collection of his essays and reviews written over a period of 40 years, from 1973 to 2013. His most recent collections of poetry are *The Cowtown Circle* (a revised and expanded edition) and *María's Book*, both published in 2016 by Alamo Bay Press. In *Texas Books in Review*, Caitlin McCrory has written that "*The Cowtown Circle* takes readers on a journey across the physical, linguistic, and metaphysical landscapes of the imagination. Dave Oliphant's poems in his latest collection look for truth by meditating on the art of others. Oliphant moves from Stephen Crane to POWs at Camp Hearne to the [Modernism of artists in] the original cowtown, Fort Worth...Throughout this collection of eclectic work, Oliphant's lines have a musicality to them, reminiscent of Langston Hughes and Fats Domino....What makes Oliphant's work so successful is his uncanny ability to get at what Tim O'Brien calls story-truth—the truth we know in our hearts." Also in *Texas Books in Review*, Zach Groesbeck has observed that "*María's Book*, a project that took forty-one years to finish, commemorates the golden wedding anniversary [of his wife's and his marriage in 1967]....The considerable time span of the collection's composition (coupled with the construction of the book) sets it apart from anything else in contemporary verse... Readers will notice Oliphant's disinterest in a sequential organization as the poems are arranged alphabetically..., rendering the book encyclopedic... [and conveying María] through her embodiment across a wider catalog of her belongings and her actions."